**Other Regal Venture
Books by Ethel Barrett**

The Strangest Thing Happened . . .
Which Way to Nineveh?
The People Who Couldn't Be Stopped

These Regal Venture books make Bible stories
come-alive for readers of every age. Also
provide exciting resources for G/L pre-teens
Bible studies.

For Family Bible storytimes
It Didn't Just Happen

The Secret Sign

BY ETHEL BARRETT

A Regal Venture Book
A Division of G/L Publications
Glendale, California, U.S.A.

Over 215,000 in print
Second Printing, 1971
Third Printing, 1973
Fourth Printing, 1974

© Copyright 1970 by G/L Publications
All rights reserved.
Printed in U.S.A.
Published by Regal Books Division, G/L Publications
Glendale, California 91209 U.S.A.

Library of Congress Catalog Card No. 78-117523
ISBN 0-8301-0008-0

The Authorized Version (King James) is the standard Bible
text for this course. Other recognized translations and
paraphrases are also used as basic supplementary tools.

Contents

A teaching and study guide for use with this book is available
from your church supplier.

The
Secret
Sign

It was happening all over. In Jerusalem. Antioch. Joppa. Ephesus. Philippi. Even in Rome itself.

The secret sign.

People whispered it to each other. Or drew it in the sand with a stick. And what was this sign?

A *fish*.

And who were the people who were using it?

The Christians in the early church.

It hadn't always been so. While Jesus was on earth, thousands of His followers had shouted His message loud and clear. They hadn't needed a secret sign then.

And then Jesus had died and had risen again and had promised to come back someday.

The followers increased and they *kept* shouting it loud and clear—for awhile.

Then there came the time when it wasn't safe to admit you were a follower of Christ. You might be thrown in prison. You might even lose your life.

Well they might have to stop shouting the gospel but they didn't stop *spreading* it.

And always there was this secret sign. Scrawled on walls and on tombs. Whispered. Written in the sand . . .

And because of this sign and the people who used it, you can hear the gospel today. They kept it alive for you. But what did the sign *mean?*

Well, the Greek word for fish was ICHTHUS. And the Greek letter for "I" was the first letter in the word "Jesus." The Greek letter for "CH" (or X) was the first letter in "Christ." "TH" was the first letter in "God." "U" was the first letter in "Son." And "S" was the first letter in "Saviour."

JESUS CHRIST—GOD'S SON—SAVIOUR

The sign was written for *you.*

This is a book about some of the people who had to use that sign, when things got tough. Some of them saw Jesus, lived with Him, talked with Him. His disciples. Zacchaeus. The woman at the well. And Mary Magdalene. And some of them never saw Him at all. Timothy. And Onesimus.

But all of them knew about the secret sign.

And all of them had many of the same problems you have today.

And they had to cope with the same kinds of "kinks" in their personalities.

So it's also a book about *you.*

CHAPTER 1

"I Always Forget What's-His-Name"

"It's the story of my life"

"People always remember the popular kids. 'Oh,' they say when they're counting noses, 'There's Steve and Paul and Mark and Mary and—then there's—uh—what's-his-name. I always forget what's-his-name.'

"And what's-his-name is *me*."

Yes it can seem like a dreary business. But if you feel this way about yourself, move over—you have lots of company. People who belong to that vast organization known as JOG.[1] The members are from everywhere. In your school, in your church, in your town, all over the world. And the members are from every generation since the beginning of time. No matter what they did, they just remained JOGS to the end of their lives.

One of them was Andrew.

[1] Just Ordinary Guys.

What? You don't know Andrew?

Well, name the disciples.

"Well—there was Peter, James and John. And Matthew, of course. And-uh—well there was Peter's brother—uh—what's-his-name. I always forget what's-his-name."

Of course.

"What's-his-name" was Andrew. He lived in Bethsaida, a tiny fishing village by Lake Galilee. No place of any importance.

He was a JOG. Just like us.

"But it isn't just where I live—it's who I have to COMPETE with"

"There's this guy[2] and he's popular—brother, is he popular! He has *everything*. He's quick to speak up, and everybody listens. He's talkative and aggressive and I'm quiet and shy. And in aptitude tests he always comes out a leader and I always come out a follower and I get so discouraged. When I listen to him and see how everybody chases after him, I just sit down and quit trying."

Well it isn't easy. But it's no reason for you to just sit down and quit. He might be "going places," but you have *your* place to go, and God knows where it is. Just ask Him. You might be surprised at how wonderful it is.

"Yeah but MY competition is right in my own family"

"I've got this brother,[3] you see, and he's everything I've always wanted to be. He talks a lot and everyone gathers around him, chases after him and when he's around, I just don't count."

[2]Or Gal—whatever. Competition is competition. Color it scary.

[3]Or sister. What's the difference? It's glum, no matter which.

You don't count? Who *says* you don't count? Nonsense. You count with God, and with God you are every bit as important as he is, and no mistake. You just have hidden talents you don't know about yet. You don't know what they are? Well ask God about them. They are diggable-uppable, and He will help you dig them up!

So get going!

Andrew had this problem. He had a brother who was so exciting, so dynamic, so talkative that wherever he went he was in the spotlight. When he talked, everybody listened. And when he said, "Let's go," everybody *went*.

Discouraging. Discouraging, indeed.

When *Andrew* said, "Let's go"—but then, Andrew never had the courage to say "Let's go."

"Okay I'm a JOG. Where do I go from here?"

Even though you're a JOG, you're still smart, and this is the natural question to ask. Where *do* you go from here? No self-respecting JOG is going to just sit around and do nothing about it. He *does* something. He *goes* somewhere.

What to do? Where to go?

"I'll go where the action is"

Naturally.

It's the thing to do. If you're a JOG, the smartest thing you can do is go where the action is.

There's only one question. And here's where you can either "make it" or fall into a trap.

Which action?

It's an important question. And the rest of your life could depend upon how you answer it.

For "which action" you choose could make the difference between going up a blind alley and batting your dumb head against a wall for the rest of your life—or going on to

3

a life with God and coming out safe and sound on the other side.

It all looks so simple when we put it this way—and we think any *idiot* ought to see it right off—and yet, so many of us JOGS just seem to run amuck right here and make the wrong choice.

Well Andrew decided to go "where the action is."

Where the real action is

And Andrew chose well. He might have been a JOG, but he was sure full of smarts.

For he chose to go where the real action was. He chose to go to Bethany where John the Baptist was preaching.

John the who? And what was he preaching?

Good questions.

Everyone wondered who he was back then, too! His doings were the gossip of the town. The country was buzzing with wild accounts of this strange man, stalking out of the hills of Judea like another Elijah, and preaching like thunder. Thousands flocked out to the desert to hear him. And the stories flew back. His garment was of camel's hair, he wore a leather girdle about his loins, he ate nothing but locusts and wild honey. And he was baptizing people in the River Jordan!

This fiery preacher had a personality that drew everyone to him. But he never talked about *himself*. He kept talking about *another* Person, so wonderful that the most exciting man on earth could not be compared with Him. " 'The man who will come after me is much greater than I am; I am not good enough even to bend down and untie his sandals!' "[4] he cried.

[4]Mark 1:7, **"Today's English Version of the New Testament."** Copyright © American Bible Society, 1966. Used by permission.

Well indeed. And *Who* could be more exciting than John the Baptist?

Andrew was very curious.

And then one day *THE MAN* walked by.

It *had* to be! For John stretched out his hand toward Him and said, "Here is the Lamb of God who takes away the sin of the world! This is the one I was talking about when I said, 'A man comes after me, but he is greater than I am, because he existed before I was born.' "⁵

The Man was Jesus Christ. He had just returned from His temptation in the wilderness.

But the Lamb of *God?*

Now Andrew was consumed with curiosity and excitement. He'd been well taught in a Jewish home; he knew of the promise of a coming Messiah. He stayed over, with his friends, to learn more. He did not have to wait long.

The very next day Jesus walked by as John was preaching, and John pointed to Him again and said, "Here is the Lamb of God!"

Now John had said it twice. Andrew was with a friend⁶ and they decided to follow Jesus and find out more.

They were trembling with excitement. Would He be hard to approach? How would they introduce themselves? But before they could muster their forces, Jesus turned to *them.*

"What are you looking for?" He asked. No wasted words. Right to the point.

"Where are you staying, Rabbi," they blurted out, all their fine speeches gone down the drain. Again, no wasted words.

"Come and see," He said simply. They followed Him meekly to where He was staying.

⁵John 1:29—31, TEV.

⁶Probably John. More about him later.

5

"This IS the real action!"

The next few hours were the most exciting ones Andrew and his friend had ever spent. They knew the prophecies—that a Messiah would come. Could He be the One? He answered every question, and taught them from the Scriptures, until there was no question about it. They even remembered the hour they'd become convinced. "It was about the tenth hour," they said later.

This man was the Messiah!

"Now at last I'm FIRST!"

If you stumbled on something great, something that suddenly made you "first"—and you knew if you shared it, you stood the chance of being knocked right back into second place again—what would you do? Keep it all to yourself? The temptation would be overwhelming.

Andrew had something at last that made him special—he'd been the first to discover the Messiah! And what did he do? He went right back to Bethsaida and told, of all people, ole Peter, his brother, the popular one, the dynamic one! Who would undoubtedly come right out and grab all the glory. Once the Messiah saw *him—!*

"Oooops—I'm back in second place again"

It is exactly what happened. Andrew hustled his brother Peter off to see Jesus. And before he could even introduce them, Jesus looked at Peter and said, "You are Simon, son of John. You shall be called Cephas, which translated is Peter—meaning stone."

Stone!

Yup, ole Peter the rock. Jesus not only knew him, but He was already prophesying that Peter would be right up there, the leader.

Andrew was back where he'd started from. Second place.

"Second place it is. So what now?"

You might be in second place but you don't have to go off and sulk about it. Andrew was the *friendliest* second-placer you'll ever read about. And being friendly is more important than being talented, if you can't be *both*.

Andrew and Peter (along with some of their friends), followed Jesus everywhere—to the wedding at Cana, to Capernaum, to Jerusalem, on to Samaria—

And then back home again to their fishing business.

It wasn't until a year later that they were confronted by Jesus again. He appeared to them on the shores of Lake Galilee while they were mending their fishing nets. And He said simply, "Follow Me. And I will make you fishers of men!"

And they did. From here on out, they belonged to the Master. Andrew's great adventure had begun.

Even a JOG can be friendly

Next time we hear about Andrew, it was about a year later. Jesus had gathered 12 disciples by then, and they were with Him as He was teaching near the shores of Lake Galilee. And what a mob there was! Five thousand men (to say nothing of the women—and children!).

Yes, children were there, and friendly ole Andrew didn't consider it beneath his dignity to be nice to them. He struck up an acquaintance with one young lad who confessed he'd brought his lunch along—five barley loaves and a couple of fishes. He was digging in for a long stay. Neither of them knew it at the moment, but that lunch was going to go down in history.

Well, the day went on and the shadows grew long and the people got restless and hungry. But still nobody wanted to leave.

And this was when that lunch suddenly became important and Andrew's friendliness paid off.

7

"How are we going to feed all these people?" Jesus asked. He asked it of one of the other disciples, who blurted out, "It would take a small fortune to feed them—at least 200 denarii!"[7]

But *Andrew* blurted out, "There's a youngster here with five barley loaves and a couple of fish!" And then as he realized what a drop in the bucket *that* would be, he added, "But what good is that with all this mob?"[8]

"Tell the people to sit down," Jesus said. The disciples marshalled the mob into groups of 100, all orderly and neat, so there'd be no confusion. And then they waited.

Jesus had only one thing to work with. He went to work on the lunch. And who brought the lunch—and the lad—to Jesus?

Friendly Andrew!

They watched in wonder as Jesus blessed the food and thanked God for it, and then began to break up the lunch and put it into baskets. And they watched in awe as the disciples passed the baskets out, each one filled to the brim —there was no *end* to the loaves and fishes—and they watched in *amazement* as the disciples collected the leftovers and there were still twelve baskets full!

Another miracle! The lunch—and the lad—and Jesus. But it was friendly Andrew who brought them all together.

Even a JOG can be generous

The next time we hear about Andrew, he was in Jerusalem and it was the last week Jesus was on earth.

It was Passover week. Jerusalem was absolutely swarming with strangers—foreigners from all over the world. The

[7]Almost a year's wages!

[8]John 6:8,9. **"The Living New Testament,"** Paraphrased (Wheaton: Tyndale House, Publishers, 1967). Used by permission.

news about Jesus and His miracles had spread abroad by this time and everyone who came to Jerusalem wanted to see Him. There were some Greeks who wanted to do more than that—they wanted to *meet* Him. "We want to meet this Jesus," they asked of one of the disciples. Now this disciple was a bit on the cautious side. Meet Jesus? Well he *knew* what most of the disciples would say. "The answer is negative," they'd say, "Tell them Jesus' ministry is to the Jews only." Who, then, to go to?

Why friendly ole Andrew!

And friendly ole Andrew knew what to do. He went with the other disciple to those Greeks, and *together* they took the foreigners to Jesus and introduced them![9]

With Andrew, *anybody* was welcome to share the good news!

"Okay, okay, but I'm just not like that!"

"I'm not only a JOG. But I'm also not the 'outgoing' type. I'm just naturally cautious. I can't help it—I was born that way."

It takes you awhile to make up your mind? You're slow to believe? You just can't push yourself forward? Hard to make decisions? "Yeah—I keep my thing locked up in my heart."

Well move over. You have lots of company.

There was a chap in the Bible just like you. Fellow by the name of Philip. Came from the same hometown Andrew did. Bethsaida. He was probably there too, listening to John the Baptist. But he didn't follow Jesus like Andrew did. He went back home, with all his longings locked in his heart; he just couldn't transfer them into his actions.

But Jesus knew Philip's heart. And Jesus found *him*.

[9]See John 12:20–22.

"Come with me," Jesus said.[10] And Philip did.

But oh, how cautiously! Do you know who the disciple was who said to Jesus, "It would take a small fortune to feed them—at least 200 denarii!"? It was Philip.

And who was too cautious and timid to take the Greeks to Jesus himself, but went to Andrew for advice?

You guessed it; it was Philip.

Philip was not only a JOG; he was a cautious and timid JOG.

But even this cautious and timid JOG had a burst of courage; he *did* do something on his very own. Right after Jesus said, "Come with me," Philip went to his best friend, Nathanael. And said, "We have found the one of whom Moses wrote in the book of the Law, and of whom the prophets also wrote. He is Jesus, the son of Joseph, from Nazareth!"[11]

And his friend gave him a hard time. "Can any good thing come from Nazareth?"[12] Nathaniel said.

And Philip, that timid JOG said, "Come and see."

And he brought his friend to Christ. So you see, the most timid cautious JOGS have their place in history.

What kind of a JOG are you?

A friendly one? A timid one? Who *says* you don't count? You count with God. You just have hidden talents you don't know about yet. You don't know what they are? Well, ask God about them. They are diggable-uppable, and He will help you dig them up!

So *get going!*

How?

[10]See John 1:43.

[11]John 1:43, 45, TEV.

[12]That hole-in-the-ground?

Well just remember—both Andrew and Philip—each in their own way—were bringing people to Jesus!

"I am the way, the truth, and the life: no man cometh unto the Father, but by me."[13]

This is the message. And this is your job, JOG.

And God speed you on your way!

[13]John 14:6.

12

CHAPTER 2

"I Gotta Be Me!"

So the song goes. Yours is a generation of searing honesty. Down with hypocrisy! Down with fakes!

"I want ♪ to ♪ beeeeee myself!" the song goes on. Be yourself. Do your thing.

We all react to different kinds of people in different ways. But on one thing we all agree; everybody hates a phony. "Be yourself!" we cry. And it's a good thing.

There's only one condition: being yourself can be good or disastrous, depending on what kind of a person you *are*. And what you are may be a long way from the kind of person God intends you to be. Take James and John, for instance—

"Oh now, WAIT a minute!"

"James and John the disciples? Why they were two of the greatest men who ever walked the earth. If I'm to follow an example, start me out on something easy. You've lost me right off, and I've hardly started the chapter. James and John are a bit too much. Why they were practically perfect."

News for you. Nobody's perfect. Nobody's even practically perfect. We're all a long way from it. And so were they.

Let's do a little poking, and see what made them tick.

James and John were brothers—sons of Zebedee. They were friends of Peter and Andrew; in fact they were partners of Peter and Andrew in the fishing business. They'd gone to hear John the Baptist too, and they'd seen Jesus.[1] They'd followed Him, too, just as Peter and Andrew had—and then they'd gone back home to tend their fishing. And a year later, they too had been interrupted from their net mending to look up into the Master's face and hear the call that turned their lives upside down.

"Follow Me."

And they'd joined the band of disciples.

And things began to happen

And from there on out, the most incredibly wonderful things happened.

Like the time they were along with the Master outside Capernaum. They'd just sailed across Lake Galilee from the country of the Gadarenes. And when they'd reached the shore, a huge crowd was waiting. And they'd got out of the boat and joined the crowd, along with Jesus—

[1]It may have been one of them who went with Andrew to see where Jesus was staying.

Sometimes they happened in public

The crowds were impossible. Jostling, pushing, demanding, pleading—they could hardly get through. And then there was this man who threw himself at Jesus' feet. Man by the name of Jairus. Leader of the Synagogue in Capernaum. His daughter was ill unto death. Would Jesus please come?

Jesus would.

He and the disciples began to push through the crowd to follow Jairus.

But what a time they had! People interrupting, people holding them back—people, people—

"Hurry," John and James thought.

And then there was this woman. Pushed her way through the crowd, scrambled to her knees at Jesus' feet and grabbed ahold of the hem of His garment. He should have brushed her off, they thought, but He didn't. He stopped. He not only stopped to look at her, but He *talked* to her. She'd been ill with an incurable disease for twelve years.

Hurry, hurry, the child is dying.

But Jesus didn't hurry.

He stopped and healed the woman.

And then some servants of Jairus elbowed their way through the crowd and said there was no need now to hurry.

The child was dead.

James and John saw Jairus' face, filled now with hopelessness. And they heard Jesus say to Jairus, "Don't be afraid—only believe."

People jostling, shouting, pushing, demanding, begging, pleading—

And Jesus turned to James and John—and Peter. And He said, "Come."

And the three of them followed Jesus and Jairus and his

servants, struggling through the crowds that would hold them back.

When they got to Jairus' home, the mourners were already wailing, the professional ones outside[2] and the real ones inside.

"Why all this confusion?" asked Jesus. "And why are you crying? The child is not dead—she is only sleeping!"[3]

They laughed Him to scorn. The child was not dead? Of course she was dead!

But Jesus brushed the mourners aside. And took John and James and Peter—inside the house with Him.

There was a dead child alright, there in her bed.

And James and John and Peter watched as Jesus walked up to the bed. And took the child's hand. And said to her, "Little lamb, get up!"

They watched as, incredibly, she opened her eyes and looked at Jesus, then stirred, then sat up—and then her wondering parents helped her out of bed, to stand, to walk—

It was another miracle!

But Jesus told them to tell nobody about it.

It did not go on record until many years later, in the gospels.

Yes, the most incredible things happened, kept happening. Like the time—a year later, when they were up on Mount Hermon—[4]

And sometimes they happened in private

It was hushed, quiet. They were alone with Him, James and John—and Peter. He had brought them up there to be

[2]In those days it was the custom to hire professional mourners.

[3]Mark 5:39, TEV.

[4]Snowcapped, 9,000 feet high. Can be seen for miles around.

alone with Him to pray. And they'd gone, struggling up the winding paths, pushing aside the straggling branches, until they'd come to a spot all quiet and peaceful—and private.

No jostling, shouting, demanding, pleading crowds. Just alone. With Jesus. To pray. It was good.

It was *too* good. James and John and Peter had had a hard day. And they got sleepy.

What a time to get sleepy!

But they did.

They had all but drowsed off, when suddenly—

All nature seemed to stand still. A great hush fell on the birds, on the trees, on the insects. Not a thing stirred. It was as if creation in that little spot had stopped in adoration. And James and John and Peter looked at Jesus in wonder.

His face was changing! It was becoming radiant with light—and His garments were blazing with light, like the sun itself! And then—

Two men appeared in heavenly splendor and majesty— Moses and Elijah! The Bible says, "Then two men appeared and began talking with Him—Moses and Elijah! They were splendid in appearance, glorious to see; and they were speaking of His death at Jerusalem, to be carried out in accordance with God's plan" (Luke 9:30, 31, LNT).

The three disciples stared, their mouths gaping open with fear and wonder. Then Moses and Elijah started to leave. And Peter found his tongue. The Bible says, as Moses and Elijah were starting to leave, Peter, all confused and not even knowing what he was saying, blurted out, "Master, this is wonderful! We'll put up three shelters—one for You and one for Moses and one for Elijah!" (verse 33).

And while Peter was still blurting, a bright cloud came down and the three disciples watched, frightened, as Jesus and Moses and Elijah disappeared into it. Then, out of the cloud, a voice. "This is my beloved Son. Listen to Him!"

The very voice of God!

17

The disciples fell to the ground on their faces in terror.

Then everything was quiet, quiet. And someone touched them on their shoulders. When they looked up, it was Jesus. He was alone. "Get up," He said simply, "don't be afraid."

It was a shattering experience. They didn't speak of it to anyone for a long, long time.

After the mountaintop, what?

What experiences! Seeing the power of Jesus in public—and being so loved, so *privileged* to see it in private too! Why James and John *must* have been "practically perfect" after experiences like those.

But they weren't. They knew the Lord alright, and intimately, but they *still* had hang-ups.

Hang-ups?

Like those crazy tempers. Why those tempers of theirs were so short, Jesus even gave them a nickname to remind them how short they were. Sometimes they really made spectacles of themselves.

Take that time they were on their way to Jerusalem with Jesus, and they wanted to use Samaria as a stopover, and the Samaritans refused to let them in the village because they were Jews—(the Samaritans and Jews were still keeping alive an old feud that started way back in the days of Nehemiah, hundreds of years before. They absolutely *hated* each other!)[5]

The other disciples took it in their stride. But James and John blew their tops. "Master, shall we order fire down from heaven to burn them up?" they bellowed.[6]

[5]You can read about this feud in the book, "Which Way to Nineveh?"
[6]Luke 9:54, LNT.

Imagine!

You get a little peeved because a few people insulted you and you want to burn up their whole *village?*

James and John did.

That nickname Jesus gave them certainly was well chosen. It was "Sons of Thunder." Sounds terrific until you consider its literal meaning: "the soon angry ones," or "sons of rage."

They must have accepted it sheepishly.

Downright embarrassing.

They had other hang-ups too.

MORE?

Like being pushy.

Jesus told them all patiently, again and again and *again* about His coming crucifixion and resurrection—that His kingdom was *not* of this earth—but for some reason they never did get it through their heads. They kept thinking that He was going to set up His kingdom here on earth—right *then.*

And of course they all wanted to get in on it—in places of honor, if possible. Most of them secretly perhaps, some of them openly. John and James made no bones about it. Sometimes it was outright embarrassing.

Take that time they came to Jesus with their mother, Mrs. Zebedee, Either they brought *her* or she brought *them.* We don't know whose idea it was. But she asked Jesus a favor. And the favor was—that her sons, James and John, would be given places of honor when Jesus set up His kingdom. To sit at His right hand and His left hand as sort of Prime Ministers, or President and Vice-President, no less.

Wow.

What kind of a woman was Mrs. Zebedee? And where was *Mr.* Zebedee while all this was going on?

And how pushy can you *get?*

What? MORE?

Like being snobs.

Take that time Jesus was right in the middle of teaching them a lesson on how to be humble, and John who was obviously not paying attention, interrupted with: "Master, we saw someone using Your name to cast out demons. And we told him not to. After all, HE ISN'T IN OUR GROUP."[7] Here Jesus was teaching a lesson in *humility* and all John could think of was: "But he's not in our *group*."

If it were today, he'd be saying, "But he isn't a Baptist!" (Or a Presbyterian or a whatever—*he doesn't have our set of rules!*)

Nice going.

"Those guys were HOPELESS!"

"Why they were *nothing*. They had lousy tempers. They were pushy. And they were snobs. And they were *disciples?*"

Yes. They were hopeless. But the most wonderful thing about them is—they *grew*.

They grew from being the "soon angry ones" to being mild-mannered. They grew from being "pushy" to being content to be the last. They grew from being "snobs" to being champions of love. Why John wrote of nothing else, in his later years: "Little children . . . love one another," he said again and again.[8]

It was John who stuck with Jesus during His arrest and crucifixion. He ran in terror at first, but he went back. It was John who ran to the empty tomb.

[7]Luke 9:49, LNT.

[8]See I, II and III John.

20

And in their later years, after Jesus had risen and gone—it was James who was killed by King Herod in Jerusalem for preaching the gospel! And it was John who was exiled from Ephesus to the isle of Patmos and wrote the book of Revelation there—and then went back to Ephesus to preach and teach and write to the end of his days.

And all he preached and taught and wrote and lived could be summed up in his words: "Little children, *love one another.*"

It was his thing.

"Wait just a minute!"

"There's one more thing. Did he really change? I mean, all through John's gospel, he refers to himself as 'the disciple Jesus loved.' That's really something. I mean, wasn't he really a bit conceited to the last?"

No.

He referred to himself as "the disciple Jesus loved"—not because he was conceited, but because he knew Jesus loved him in spite of all his faults. He remembered his temper, his pushiness, his snobbishness. He remembered it well.

But he remembered too, how he had grown under Jesus' teaching, Jesus' love, Jesus' understanding, Jesus' patience.

He remembered, he remembered . . .

"I gotta be me!"

Of course.

And God wants you to be *you.* There's nobody quite like you in all the world. And so, naturally, you must be *yourself.* Not a phony. There's only one condition: being yourself can be good or disastrous, depending on what kind of a person you *are.* And what you are may be a long way from the kind of person God intends you to be.

Why don't you put yourself in His hands?

21

List your shortcomings (and you won't be alone; we all have them). Be perfectly honest with yourself, and with God.

And let Him teach you, help you *grow*.

You can still be *you—but a better you*.

Like John and James. And remember the verse: "Not by works of righteousness which we have done, but according to his mercy he saved us, by the washing of regeneration, and renewing of the Holy Ghost."[9]

It's God Who does the work!

He did it with John and James.

He can do it with you.

[9]Titus 3:5.

23

CHAPTER 3

"It's Gotta Be Real!"

"Tell it like it is"

So the saying goes. It has become the hue and cry of
your generation. "Don't gloss it over—give it to us straight!
The world's a mess and everything seems absolutely hopeless. So quit pretending. Tell it like it is.

"*Realism.* That's the thing. Nothing but what I can see
here and now. And 'nothing but the facts, ma'am.' "

It's an extremely intelligent outlook on life. But like
every good thing, it has its pitfalls if it's carried too far.

There was a man back in Jesus' time who would have fit
right into your generation; you'd have considered him right
up-to-date. Name of Thomas. Yes, he was one of the disciples. *That* one. *Doubting Thomas.* His name is a household
word.

"That's not fair!"

"Now you're bringing out all my guilt complexes. Because I have a lot of honest questions about God. But I'm afraid to speak up because it makes me look like some kind of dum-dum. All the really great Christians I know never seem to have any doubts at all. They seem to have gotten ahold of something I've missed. So I keep my questions to myself, for fear my parents and everyone will think I'm going to the dogs or something."

You are not alone

Cheer up. In the first place, honest questions—and even honest doubts—don't make you a dum-dum. In the second place, even the greatest Christians have had their doubts. Even John Bunyan—and he was one of the greatest Christians who ever lived[1]—confessed that he was plagued all his life by secret doubt. His faith sometimes had a pretty hard time of it.

You have lots of company

"Okay—other great Christians maybe. But other *disciples* besides Thomas? Name one!"

Easy.

When Mary Magdalene saw Jesus in the garden alive—after He'd been crucified and was dead and buried—she dashed off to find the disciples and tell them the astounding news. And they, after Mary told them that Jesus was alive, and that she had seen Him, *didn't believe it!*[2]

And later, when those two disciples on their way to Emmaus saw Him and talked with Him—and then dashed

[1] He wrote "Pilgrim's Progress."
[2] Read Mark 16:11.

back to tell the others—"again *no one believed them.*"[3]

And still later, Jesus upbraided all eleven of the other disciples[4] for their unbelief!

Name one?

"I'll go along with it—but it won't be easy"

With our hearts we know that God is in complete control of the universe. "Great is Thy faithfulness, O God my Father," we sing, "Sun, moon and stars in their courses above—"

But our pesky *minds* keep getting in the way. One looks at the world, at wars, at riots, and all the mischief *man* has in store for us, and all is gloom again. And we go right back to, "Don't gloss it over—tell it like it is!"

In Bunyan's *Pilgrim's Progress,* there's a man with a muck-rake. He's all stooped over, looking down, raking up stones and sticks and dust. There's a glorious light above him, the very God Himself, but the man does not see. He's too busy raking muck. Bunyan says the sticks and stones and dust are the things of this world—the junky things that don't count. But they could also be our doubts and fears. We rake them up and coddle them, indeed they become so much a part of our thinking that we can't take our eyes off them.

Well when it came to raking up doubts, Thomas was a first-rate muckraker.

Like that time Jesus got word from Mary and Martha that their brother Lazarus was very ill. Would Jesus come to Bethany at once?

Now Mary and Martha and Lazarus were Jesus' most beloved friends. The obvious thing to do was to go. There was only one hitch.

[3]See Mark 16:13.

[4]Mark 16:14. Thomas wasn't there, or he'd have caught it too.

Bethany was in Judea, and in Judea, Jesus was in trouble. The Jewish leaders there had threatened to stone Him; Bethany was, humanly speaking, "off limits."

So when Jesus said, "Let's go back to Judea," the disciples were all horrified. "But the Jews are threatening to stone you—are you going back there again?"

Thomas raked away at his doubts. It was a dangerous thing to do, going to Bethany. They'd all surely be killed. And then, *still raking away at his doubts*, he cried, "Let's all go to Bethany and die with Him!"

Woweeeee! Thomas, in that moment, became ten feet tall! It's one thing to go on when things seem hopeless, when you're believing in the power of God—but to go on when you're up to your eyeballs in doubts—*that* kind of plowing on takes some doing! It's like saying, "I haven't any faith at the moment, but I'll go along with it anyway." Or like the man in Mark's gospel,[5] who cried out, "Lord, help my unbelief!" Or like saying, "I'm really not with it, but I'll go along anyway, until I see some light!"

For Thomas to go along with Jesus[6] *in spite* of all his doubts is a blazing example for all us doubters, right up to this day.

It paid off, too. Thomas plowed on, and he *did* find the light. But first . . .

Questions, questions!

There was a letter in the *Los Angeles Times*, a real letter from a child to God. It said simply: "Dear God: Are you for real?"

The same thing occurred to Thomas, many times. He

[5]See Mark 9:24.

[6]They did go to Bethany and Jesus raised Lazarus from the dead. You can read the thrilling story in John 11:1—46.

thought that Jesus was going to set up His kingdom right then and there, on earth. But that was no disgrace; so did the other disciples. Jesus kept telling them that He would die for the sins of the world, that He would rise again—that He would go away, and leave the Holy Spirit to stay while He was gone—

He told them and told them, but they could not comprehend it. On that day He rode into Jerusalem in triumph[7] and the people sang and cheered and greeted Him as a king—they thought sure that would be His coronation day, that He would set up His kingdom.

But He did not.

And Thomas brooded and wondered and doubted. There with his muck-rake, raking his doubts, his head down. Forever down. "Are you for real?"

"I don't know what You're up to, Lord!"

No, you often don't. It can be the agony of being a Christian—or the surprise and challenge and glory of being a Christian—depending on which way you're looking at it. It can be: "What are You up to *now?*"—glum, glum, rake away at those doubts. Or it can be: "Woweee! What are You up to *now?* Whatever it is, I know it's for my own good. Surprise me!"

And it's suddenly a great adventure, with a surprise and a miracle at every turn of the road!

And Thomas? Raking away, poor chap. He just couldn't take his eyes off his muck-rake.

Next time we hear about him, they were all in the upper room, Jesus and the disciples, for their last Passover supper.

It was a dramatic moment. Jesus had just said that one of them would betray Him. And Judas had left suddenly and plunged out into the night.

[7]Palm Sunday.

"I'll be with you for only a little while longer," Jesus said to the rest.

Thomas listened, brooding.

"You will look for Me—but where I go, you cannot follow." He went on.

Silence. Despair. It hung in the room, like a cloud.

"Love one another," He said. "By this all men will know that you are My disciples—"

"Well, what was this? What does this have to do with my problem?"

If you're asking it, they were asking it too.

"—if you love one another—" Jesus went on.

"Where are you *going?*" Peter interrupted.

He echoed Thomas' question; Thomas' throat was too dry to ask. Love one another? It was beside the point. Where *was* He going? What was He *up* to?

"Where I'm going, you cannot follow Me now. But you will follow Me later."

What, WHAT?

"I go to prepare a place for you," Jesus went on. "And I'll come again, and take you to be with Me."

WHAT?

"—and you know where I am going and how to get there."

By this time, Thomas had all his doubts raked up into one big pile.

"No—" he interrupted, "We *don't* know where you're going—so how can we know how to get there?"

Well! It was like a bombshell.

It opened a barrage of questions from the other disciples. Thomas had his poor little doubts raked up into one big pile, and he came right out with them, and he found that others had questions too!

They asked, and Jesus answered.[8] *He* is the way. He had to leave them. He would send the Holy Spirit to them. And He would come back. Meanwhile, they had work to do. He explained it all.

Thomas listened. But he did not comprehend.

"I'm all in shambles"

"It's no use. I just don't understand it all. I'm going to quit."

So you don't understand it? And you're going to quit reading your Bible? And turn your hearing aid down when you go to Sunday School?

Well, watch it. You just might miss something very important—that could change your life.

Thomas did.

He stayed away.

He fled in fear during the crucifixion. He stayed away when the other disciples met in the upper room on the night of the Resurrection Day. And what he missed!

They all exchanged what they had experienced. The tomb had been empty! Jesus had appeared to Mary Magdalene! And to two of the disciples on their way to Emmaus! And then, suddenly—even while they were talking—

Right through a locked door—Jesus Himself appeared to them! At first they thought He was a ghost, but He showed them the prints of the nails in His hands and the wound in His side!

Thomas didn't see it. He wasn't there. He'd turned his hearing aid off.

And when they told him all about it, he said, "Unless I see in His hands the print of the nails, and place my finger

[8]Read John 14 and 15.

31

in the mark of the nails, and place my hand in His side, I will not believe."[9]

"I just can't believe other people's experiences!"

"I've got to see for myself. If this thing is real—then it's got to be real for *me.*"

Of course. And it *should* be.

The idea is, you keep going back, until it *is*. In spite of all your doubts, if you're "for real" with God—He'll be "for real" with you.

He has promised you this. And He will *not* fail you.[10]

Your pile of muckraked doubts is pretty high?

So was Thomas'. *Very* high.

But he went back.

A week later he went back, and it is much to his credit, for his pile of doubts was up over his eyeballs.

It was in the upper room. You see, he went back to the place where the real action was.

It's a good place to be, in spite of all your doubts.

It pays off.

It paid off for Thomas.

For suddenly—

"It's for real!"

Through the locked doors (and over all the doubts) Jesus Himself appeared again!

And He looked right at Thomas.

"Put your finger into My hands. Put your hand into My side. Don't be faithless any longer. Believe!"[11]

---

[9]See John 20:25, RSV.

[10]See Jeremiah 29:13 and Joshua 21:45.

[11]John 20:27, LNT.

The exact words Thomas had said!

Woosh, went the muckrake. Down went the pile of doubts. Thomas finally knew. He *knew*.

"My Lord and my God," he said.

This is for you

There's one more verse there. And it's for you. It's what Jesus answered Thomas—and it is this:

"Have you believed because you have seen Me? Well, happy are those who have *not* seen, and still believe."

It's for you, right down the line. To this very day.

"But I've still got this pile of doubts here"

Sure. And you're busy raking them up with your muckrake. Into a huge pile.

What are your questions?
"Who am I?" (Genesis 1:26; 9:6)
"Where did I come from?" (John 1:3)
"How should I feel toward God?" (Psalm 107:8)

And then, some answers:

God's love doesn't change (Romans 8:35-37)
All of us will face a time of judgment (Hebrews 9:27)
We have eternal life through Christ (I John 5:13)
Peace with God (Romans 5:1)
Help in time of trouble (II Corinthians 4:8-10)
Answers to prayers (I John 5:14,15)
We shall live after death (Philippians 3:21)
We shall be like Christ (I John 3:2)
A crown of righteousness (II Timothy 4:7,8)

And after all the questions, learn this:

"These things have I written unto you that believe on the name of the Son of God; that ye may know that ye have eternal life, and that ye may believe on the name of the Son of God" (I John 5:13).

Believe on the Son of God. Your questions will be answered, as you go along.

Stick with it!

CHAPTER 4

"Sometimes I Feel Like a Reject"

"They say I'm reaching the age when only a mother could love me, and sometimes she has her doubts. It sounds funny when you say it but it isn't funny really. I wouldn't admit it if I had to sign my name or anything, but I secretly feel that people don't like me, and that I'm sort of worthless."

You do, do you? Well you're not alone. More people feel "sort of worthless" than this world dreams of. And more often than not, the "gap" they feel between themselves and other people, is purely imaginary. Or if it's really there, it's of their own making. "Teachers!" they say. "They hate me!"

Or, "My brothers and sisters! Yaaauk!" Or, "I get along with my friends okay—but oh my *parents*."

Like in the song—

> Nobody likes me,
> Everybody hates me,
> I'm going to the backyard
> And eat wooly worms.

—they jump to the conclusion that they are rejected and go off in a snit without thinking it through.

"Smile when you say that!"

"With most kids it might be in their imagination, but with me it's for real. And it isn't funny."

You may be right. For the painful truth is, some parents *don't* care. Or other people, either. And whether you're loose on the streets or cozy in a church, rejection is painful beyond words to describe. And there's one thing for you to remember:

God loves rejects! And He always has!

Some of the people He sought out and asked to follow Him, were some of the biggest rejects in society!

Take Matthew, for instance.

Nobody loved a tax collector!

When your father begins to talk to himself, bump into furniture, and absent mindedly call you "Exemption" instead of by your name, you know it's that time of year again.

Income tax.

And when you buy something that is priced at $1.98 and it turns out to be $2.16, you know what the culprit is. The tax.

So you have some idea of what taxes are. But you know

they are necessary to run things and you know they are set on a percentage basis, and not by somebody's whim.

Not so, back in Jesus' time.

Taxes were set by tax collectors who paid the government (the highest bidder got the job) fat sums for their tax-collecting permit. The idea was, they'd collect taxes from the people, turn over the proper percentage of it to the government, and keep the rest for themselves. Nothing wrong with that. A chap has to make a living. And if these chaps had done just that, they would have been respectable members of society.

But they charged outrageously above what was right and proper, and pocketed the difference themselves. If the fellow being taxed couldn't afford to pay, the tax collector had an answer for that one, too. He loaned the money at an exorbitant rate of interest so the poor chap paid twice the amount before he was through.

In short, they robbed the people blind.

So you see, they weren't very popular.

Nobody liked a tax collector but *another* tax collector.

Especially a Jewish tax collector!

Now it was quite bad enough for anybody to go into this business—but for a Jew! A Jew to work for the enemy oppressors, to rob people, including his own people—blind? A *Jew*?

But some Jews did.

And they were most despised of all people, among other Jews. Not only because they were dishonest, but because their work brought them into daily contact with *Gentiles*.

A Jewish tax collector?

Ugh!

And you guessed it. Matthew was a Jewish tax collector. Which made him just about as big a reject as you could find.

He worked in Capernaum, a profitable place to set up business. It was near the highway that led from Damascus to the coastal cities. And it was on the Sea of Galilee. So taxes could be collected on goods shipped by road or sea. He had it "made."

It was also the area where Jesus lived and preached.

Matthew must have heard the Master teach. He must have talked with Him. He may have even collected Jesus' taxes! Can you imagine Matthew, there in his tax collector's booth, giving Jesus His change (What change?—those fellows kept it all) and looking down at his books while they were talking, ashamed to meet the Master's eyes? Can you imagine the good things of the Lord he tucked away in his heart? And the struggle he had with his conscience?

And then that great day when Jesus walked up to Matthew's booth and said, "Now, Matthew, this is a day of decision. I want you to leave all this—and follow Me."

Amazing! The great reject was being called to the Lord!

Matthew made his great decision without quibbling. The Bible says, "And Matthew jumped up and went along with Him."[1]

From this description, it looks like ole Matthew hardly took time to gather up his books or wind up his business! He even gave a dinner party at his home and invited all his friends (the most notorious swindlers in town) to meet his new Master!

From that moment on, he followed our Lord—and his pen and ink were never used again to juggle accounts and rob people blind—they were used to take down all he could of what Jesus did and said. How do we know? Well who do you suppose wrote the Gospel of Matthew?

Of course.

The old reject.

[1]Matthew 9:9, LNT.

He was confronted by the Master, made his decision, and swept into full-time service, all in one fell swoop!

"Now you've lost me!"

"It always seems like you're *nobody* if you don't go into 'full-time service'.[2] Isn't every Christian in 'full-time service'?[3] When missionaries come home and say, 'Then, when I *really* gave myself to the Lord, I became a missionary.' And then I always feel like a heel. Does all this mean that if I don't go into full-time service I don't really love the Lord?"

Good question.

And there's a good answer. Let's take another reject. Let's take Zacchaeus.

You know the story well; you probably cut your teeth on it. Zacchaeus was the little short chap who wanted to see Jesus so badly. But he got jostled in the crowd and elbowed out of the way. And there was nothing in front of him but heads, heads, heads. He couldn't see a thing. So he ran up the road (this happened in Jericho) and climbed up into a Sycamore tree where he'd have a vantage point when Jesus came by. *Now* he'd see the Master, and he felt so smart about it all that he quite forgot the ridicule he was subjecting himself to. After all, he was a well-known figure in the city of Jericho. You guessed it; he was a chief tax collector!

In all the hubbub about Zacchaeus did you ever stop to think (when you were very young) what he *was*? A tax collector! What if he got caught?

He did. In the most astounding way. It wasn't that any of his friends caught him—it was that the *Master Himself* caught him.

---

[2] Be a minister or a missionary, etc.

[3] Yes!

There he was, safe and carefully hidden in the branches of the Sycamore tree, looking down—waiting.

And the Master came by. And looked up. Right at Zacchaeus. And everybody *else* looked up, too.

Oh good grief.

Zacchaeus' world stood still. He was undone.

And then two absolutely astounding things happened.

The Master looked up at Zacchaeus—and said—"Zacchaeus—"

The Master called him by name!

"Quick! Come down! For I am going to be a guest in your home today!"[4]

The Master wanted a *personal relationship* with him!

Earthshaking!

Zacchaeus' little world spun around and came to a standstill. The *Lord Himself* wanted a personal relationship with *him?*

Yes indeed.

Well little Zacchaeus shimmied down that Sycamore tree so fast, he might have slivers to show for it today in heaven.[5]

And, sure enough, that very day he entertained the Master in his home!

But did he go into full-time service?

No.

He apparently wasn't called to do this. He was called to go back about his business, but now as an honest man. For the Bible tells us—"Sir," said Zacchaeus, "I will give half my belongings to the poor. And if I've cheated anyone—[6] why, I'll give him back four times as much!"[7]

---

[4]Luke 19:5, LNT.

[5]For you can bet he's there!

[6]He **knew** he had, the rascal!

[7]It was an old law of Moses; if you stole anything you gave back four times as much, and no nonsense.

And Jesus said back: "This shows that salvation has come to this home today. This man was one of the lost sons of Abraham, and I, the Son of Mankind, have come to search for and to save *such souls as his.*"[8]

Now Matthew followed Jesus as a disciple and as an apostle, in full-time service. And Zacchaeus followed Jesus as a good and honest Christian, *not* in "full-time service." But they both belonged to Jesus, and had a *personal relationship* with Him.

And one was just as good a Christian as the other.

"But what has this to do with me?"

"Bring it down to today—so I can understand."

Well, there is Don Moomaw of all-American football fame, planned to go with the Rams. But he planned "if the Lord wants me to." It turned out that the Lord wanted him to preach the gospel instead, and he obeyed. Like Matthew. It's where he is now.

And then there's Cazzie Russell of all-American basketball fame. He planned to stay in basketball "if the Lord wants me to"—and that's exactly where the Lord wanted him to stay. And Cazzie's ministry is "witnessing." He's known for his bull sessions in the Knickerbocker locker room, witnessing to the other members on his team. He's also known for his "disciplined practice and his tremendous *enthusiasm.*" Like Zacchaeus.

It turned out the Lord wanted Matthew to go into full-time service and He wanted Zacchaeus to just stay where he was, only now a blazing light, an example to all. And one was as great a Christian as the other!

So what are you stewing about?

The really *important* thing is—do you, or do you not, have a *personal* relationship with Jesus Christ?

Well?

[8]Luke 19:9, 10, LNT.

The vultures are coming, the vultures are coming

And, to be sure, they did.

And who were the vultures?

The Pharisees! Those look-down-your-nose-and- watch-it-I'm-a-better-Christian-than-you-are- people who, in those days, knew all the laws, and knew all the answers but one. And that one was love.

Love? They didn't know what it was. They just weren't *with* it.

And so, when Matthew gave his party for Jesus, they gathered outside and criticized and asked the disciples— "What's going on in there? And why does your teacher eat with tax collectors and outcasts?"

And Jesus heard them. And He had an answer. "People who are well do not need a doctor, but only those who are sick. Go and find out what this scripture means, 'I do not want *animal* sacrifices, but kindness.' For I have not come to call the respectable people, but the outcasts."[9]

He was quoting a verse from their own Old Testament![10]

"For it is goodness I want," He was saying— "not sacrifice. It is the knowledge of God—a personal relationship with Him—it is *love!*"[11]

And did the Pharisees ever learn? Well, when Zacchaeus entertained the Lord in his home, the Pharisees were still in a stew (and it was two years later!)[12]—and what did they do but grumble to the disciples—"This man has gone as a guest to the home of a sinner!"

We have no record of what Jesus said in reply to this—

[9]Matthew 9:12, 13, TEV. And by "respectable" people, He meant "self-righteous."

[10]See Hosea 6:6.

[11]Read Hosea 6:6—you'll be astounded!

[12]Two years after Matthew's party.

but it's a pretty good guess that He told them the same thing. It was not sacrifice He wanted—it was love.

"What's the point?"

Well there are two points. One is—are you a reject? (Or do you feel like one; it's the same thing.) Well, will you believe, right now, that God loves you—that Jesus Christ loves you—that He wants you for Himself—whether you go into "full-time service" or just go on about your business, being a witness for Him?

And are you ready for the vultures? Will you let them just squash you down, or will you stick with it and let the Lord take care of you? Will you show them love when they don't know enough to show *you* love?

It takes a bit of doing.

Or are *you* a "vulture"?

"Me? A VULTURE?"

"Oh, perish forbid! Why I've gone to Sunday School all my life—I know all the rules and all the answers—what do you *mean*—'are you a vulture?' "

You and your conscience[13]

YOUR CONSCIENCE: Come off it.

YOU: What do you mean, come off it?

CONSCIENCE: I mean, come off it. What do *you* do with the "rejects" in your class?

YOU: They seem kinda crumby. I mean, they're *outsiders*.

CONSCIENCE: Outsiders, are they? What did Jesus do with Matthew and Zacchaeus? *They* were outsiders. And what did Jesus say to the self-righteous Pharisees?

---

[13]You are not reading this book alone. Your conscience is looking over your shoulder.

45

YOU: They're kinda crumby. I mean the "rejects" in my class.

CONSCIENCE: You're getting off the groove. What *did* Jesus do with Matthew and Zacchaeus?

YOU: He used them both. One in public service; one in private life. They were both terrific.

CONSCIENCE: And what did He say to the Pharisees?

YOU: He told them off.

CONSCIENCE: Well?

YOU: You make *me* feel like a heel.

CONSCIENCE: You *are* a heel.

YOU: I mean, they *were* terrific. Both of them. They both turned out better than any of the Pharisees did.

CONSCIENCE: Well?

YOU: *I'm* a heel.

CONSCIENCE: You sure are.

"What's for me?"

Well, if you're a "reject"—just know that God loves you, and try to put up with the Pharisees.

And if you're a "Pharisee"—you just might be lower, in God's eyes, than a "reject."

So watch it.

And you just might memorize Romans 14:13: "Then let us no more criticize *and* blame *and* pass judgment on one another, but rather decide *and* endeavor never to put a stumbling block *or* an obstacle or a hindrance in the way of a brother."[14]

Do you good.

[14]"The Amplified Bible." (Grand Rapids: Zondervan Publishing House, 1965). Used by permission.

You must view that people in different ways because of cultural appearance.

CHAPTER 5

"Me? A Phony?"

What kind of a person are you?

It's one of the titles you see on the covers of magazines under "SPECIAL FEATURES IN THIS ISSUE." Or it might be called "What Kind of an Employee Are You?" or "Are You Really a Good Sport?" or "Is Your Marriage a Success?"[1] or "Are You Capable of Friendship?" or

---

[1] You're not ready for that one yet, and no fair checking on your parents.

"Which is the real you?"

These tests are always compiled by some leading psychologist from We-Find-U-Out University. And we love to take them, for we have a sneaking desire to see what we're *really* like. And we jot our answers down in pencil and erase them after we've added up our score, so the rest of the family *won't* find out.

There's nothing like one of those tests to either prove to us what angels we really are (and if the test proves you an angel, you fudged a little), or bring us up with a jolt.

Personality tests in the Bible?

There's a book in the New Testament that is filled with these personality tests. It wasn't written by a psychologist from any We-Find-U-Out University. It was written by James, and he "finds you out" in almost every verse.

Who James? Why the head of the early church at Jerusalem. If you'd lived back in those times, you'd have heard him discussed near the Sheep Gate of Jerusalem, or in the funny crooked streets, or in the shade of the Temple porches, or in the Court of the Gentiles within the Temple itself.

For he was an immensely important and influential man —known as "James the Just." When he spoke people listened, and when he said "jump" people said "how high?"

The book of James is really a letter James wrote to the Jewish Christians who had been scattered into the provinces by persecution, by circumstances, by hardship. The letter was to buck them up, bawl them out, remind them of both their privileges and responsibilities, and, in general, jolt them out of their doldrums and into reality.

And what a thundering letter it is! He leaps without apology from one subject to another, and a "personality test" could be compiled on any subject he covers.

But, no matter *what* subject he covers, the whole letter is

an outraged cry against the great bugaboo of Christianity
—*hypocrisy*.

It's a great roaring letter written by a great roaring man.
And it all boils down to—

What kind of a phony are *you?*

There's no room here to take up *all* the subjects—but
let's try on a few for size. For a starter, let's take your atti-
tude toward people.

"Me? Why I like EVERYBODY"

Do you?

Well, what would you do with this personality test:

When you walk into a group which would you be most
apt to do? (1) Go talk to the best-dressed person in the
room. (2) Look for your own little clique and stick with it.
(3) Seek out some lonely looking kook and talk with him.
(4) Stop and talk to a stranger and try to draw him into
the group. (5) Go sit in a corner and look bored. (6) Try
to "take over" the group by being the life of the party, and
stick with only the people who respond. (7) Leave, if nobody pays any attention to you. (8) Ignore anyone in the
room who seems to be in authority. (The "sponsors" will do
for a start.) (9) Or if you see someone *you* have some authority over, go over and browbeat him.

Or when you meet a person, how do you size him up?
(1) Pride yourself on making "snap judgments" and decide
whether he's "in" or "out" right on the spot. (2) Decide
he's "out" because his skin is a different color. (3) Look at
his clothes and put a mental price tag on them and judge
him accordingly. (4) Dismiss him and move on if he seems
dull. (5) Be nice to him and reserve your judgment. (6)
Decide he's okay if he's popular. (7) Snub him if he's
"stuck-up." (8) Treat him with with suspicion if he's in authority.

James has a few things to say that might help you evaluate your answers:

"How can you claim to be a Christian," he roars, "and show favoritism to rich people and look down on poor people? If one person comes into your church well dressed and another comes in poorly dressed, and you fuss over the well-dressed one and ignore the poor one—aren't you making class distinctions? And aren't you setting yourself up as a judge?[2] This is a no-no!"

And that's only a starter. You can also be snobs about people who are dull, and fawn over people who are popular. Or you can feel inferior, sort of as if you belonged to a minority group, and go off and sulk and *snub the snobs.* There are so many ways to have wrong attitudes and use snap judgment about people, the list would go on forever. And they're all no-nos!

James sums up the whole bit this way: "My brothers! In your life as believers in our Lord Jesus Christ, the Lord of glory, you must never treat people in different ways *because of their outward appearance.*"[3] And that means more than just looks and clothing. It means the "outward appearance" of their *behavior* too.

Do you like everybody? Or do you like everybody it's convenient and profitable to like?

So much for your attitudes. Now a bit about your tongue.

"Me? Why I'm just all sweet talk"

Try this little personality test:

When you hear a bit of scandal about someone, which are you apt to do? (1) Tell everybody in sight. (2) Tell

[2]Read James 2:1–4.

[3]James 2:1, TEV.

just a few people in confidence. (3) Tell only your best friend so the two of you can share it. (4) Keep it to yourself and pray for that person. (5) Go to the person and demand to know if it's true.

There are many ways you can bungle with your tongue, and we'll get to them in a minute. But first, let's see what James has to say about it. And he has plenty to say in chapter three.

Teeny little spark; heap big fire

"The tongue is very small," he says, "but what a lot of damage it can do! Why a whole forest can be set afire by one tiny spark!"[4]

He compares the harm the tongue can do with one of the most treacherous destroyers known to man. We get acquainted with it early in our childhood. It's one of the first no-nos.

There was a true account in a newspaper about a child on a camping trip. He was sent to the foot of the camp to empty some rubbish. As he was going through some brush, a small animal scampered by and rustled the bushes. The child's father heard him whisper, "Is that you, Smokey?" We're taught to dread fire and prevent it as soon as we can understand.

James says the tongue is every bit as dangerous. A careless word, a nasty rumor, a bit of slander—and you've started a fire that's out of control, for the harm you've done is *done*—and you can't get the "spark" back.

Sure the tongue is small. So is a bit in a horse's mouth.[5] But with that bit you can steer a horse down the bridle path where he's supposed to go, or you can steer him into a

[4]Read James 3:5.

[5]Read James 3:3.

tree and he'll hang you up on a limb. For your tongue can not only hurt others. It can trip *you* up too. For James says "it can poison the whole body; it can make our whole lives into a blazing disaster."[6]

There are ways and ways

For your tongue to trip you up, that is. The list is a long one. Do you "exaggerate a little"? Do you use "strong language"? Is your "wit" a bit on the sarcastic side? Does it bother you to hurt other peoples' feelings, or does it give you a bit of a kick? You can add a few of your own. You'll need a lot of paper.

"But I don't say nasty things"

No, but you might *look* them. And sometimes a look says more than a thousand words.

The Look of Sudden Death. This is a frozen stare. It's the "if looks could kill" look.

The Dead Pan. This look resembles fish on chipped ice in the meat market. It's sometimes used on teachers. It means you don't want to communicate and are making no bones about it.

The Martyr's Mask. This is a look of extreme pain. Biting the lower lip helps. Tears, if this fails. It's used on parents when you can't borrow ahead on next week's allowance.

The Resigned Look. The eyes are rolled back. The mouth moves but no sound comes out. A big sigh helps here. It's often used when parents tell you to clean your room for the fifteenth time.

And you think you're not saying anything because you're not using your tongue? You're saying *plenty*.

[6]See James 3:6.

And James says, "Watch it!"
FOR "NO HUMAN BEING CAN TAME THE TONGUE."[7]

"WELL then, it all looks hopeless"

Well it *is* a battle—but not a losing one. For God can help you control the little monster. *Ask* Him to help you. Try this every morning: "Let the words of my mouth, and the meditation of my heart (this will take care of those "looks"), be acceptable in thy sight, O LORD, my strength, and my redeemer."[8]

It works!

So much for your tongue. Now about your temptations.

"Temptations? I handle them my own way"

Do you?

Try this personality test:

When you're tempted to do wrong, do you: (1) Jump at the chance. (2) Decide to just *think* about it without doing it. (3) Go talk it over with your best friend, hoping he'll give you some good reason for doing it. (4) Try to fight it out by yourself. (5) Take it to God.

James says take it to God. "So give yourself humbly to God. Resist the devil and he will flee from you. And when you draw close to God, God will draw close to you. . . ."[9]

In John Bunyan's story of *Pilgrim's Progress*, "Christian,"[10] who is making his way through the journey of life, meets Satan on the way. "Where have you come from," said Satan, "and where d'you think you're going?"

[7]Read James 3:8, LNT.
[8]Read Psalm 19:14.
[9]James 4:7, 8, LNT.
[10]The hero of the story.

"I've come from the world," said Christian, "and I'm on my way to heaven. I belong to the King!"

"Oh come, come," said Satan, "it's common for those who call themselves Christians to give Him the slip after awhile and return again to me. Why don't you do it too?"

"But I *want* to follow Him!"

Satan tried another tack. "You've already been unfaithful to Him," he said, "and do you think He wants you now?" And he proceeded to name a long list of Christian's failures, in every humiliating detail.

"Everything you say is true," said Christian when Satan had finished, "and there's more that you left out. But my King is merciful and ready to forgive. And give me strength to resist you."

Then Satan broke out in a rage. "I hate this King of yours!" he roared, "I hate His laws—I hate His people! And I've come on purpose to make you fall!"

"Beware of what you do," said Christian, "for I'm in the King's highway: watch it!"

The battle that followed was terrible to see. Satan straddled the highway in front of Christian and his evil darts flew as thick as hail. Christian fought with all his might, and then—

He dropped his sword![11]

And down he went!

He lay on the ground exhausted and Satan nearly did him in. *Nearly.*

For Christian reached for his sword, managed to get ahold of it, and CAME UP SWINGING!

"When I fall, I shall arise!"[12] he shouted and WHAP!— gave Satan a deadly thrust and the culprit fled!

Resist Satan—and he will flee from you!

[11]THE SWORD IS THE WORD OF GOD!

[12]See Micah 7:8.

Go back and look at the "personality test" again. How do you rate now?

That's not all there is—there's more

But there isn't room to tell it here. The book of James is filled with enough "personality tests" to keep psychologists from We-Find-U-Out University happy for years.

For James "finds you out" in every verse.

James—head of the early church in Jerusalem. And do you know who else James was?

"Phonies" can come from the nicest places"

He was our Lord's *brother!*

Yes. Actually. His "born-and-brought-up" brother. Jesus was Mary's son by the Holy Spirit of God. But after Jesus was born, as the angel had promised, Mary and Joseph had other children—and James was one of them.[13] He ate at the same table with Jesus, worked in the same carpenter's shop with Him, played with Him. When Jesus went to Jerusalem for His first Passover when He was twelve years old, James probably waited eagerly to hear all about the service. He *grew up* with Him. But did he believe Jesus is the Son of God?

There isn't a clue in the Bible that he did. How many times James must have been scandalized at the things his brother was doing! Hobnobbing with that no-good Zacchaeus, turning water into wine at Cana, calling another tax collector (Matthew) to be His disciple, eating with publicans and sinners, stopping to chat with a *Samaritan* woman by a well. And preaching such strange doctrines! Why once James hustled over to Capernaum with his

---

[13]Read Mark 6:3. James' name always appears first in the list of brothers and sisters, so he was probably the eldest.

mother and brothers and sisters when they heard that Jesus was not only teaching strange doctrines, but wasn't eating or sleeping. Outrageous! Everyone thought He was mad! "Get Him out of here," they thought, "and take Him home."[14]

James must have spent a lot of time apologizing for his brother Jesus. Right up until His dreadful crucifixion.

And we haven't a clue that James was even there.

And then our Lord rose from the dead. And "He was seen of James." Paul tells us this.[15] Nothing more. The rest is locked in mystery. Jesus was seen of James somewhere, and whatever happened, James was sent spinning, his life never to be the same again. Jesus was never just his brother again; Jesus was his *Lord*.

A life spun around

Much later, on Paul's first visit to Jerusalem, he said he stayed with Peter. "And the only other apostle I met at that time was James, our Lord's brother."[16]

Apostle!

Yes, James had joined the great organization of the secret sign.

And still later there was a big hullabaloo in the early church[17] as to whether Gentiles could become Christians. "Not unless they follow the Jewish laws first!" cried some. "Salvation is only for the Jews!" But a wise leader stood up in the council meeting and said, "Let them in. The gospel is for everybody."

[14]Read Mark 3:21, 31, 32.

[15]I Corinthians 15:7.

[16]Galatians 1:19, LNT.

[17]You can read about it in "The People Who Couldn't Be Stopped," a Regal Venture Book.

What wise leader?

James!

James had stopped being just "religious." And he'd stopped being a phony. He was now a follower of the Way.

"Me? A phony?"

Well, are you?

One of the most important verses in James' letter is: "But be ye doers of the word, and not hearers only, deceiving your own selves."[18]

Now how do you stack up?

[18]James 1:22.

CHAPTER 6

"But Nobody's as Bad as I Am!"

Or nobody is as insecure, or as "left out" or as misunderstood, or as dumb, or as ugly, or as unpopular. These are only some of the things most of us secretly feel about ourselves, though we'd rather have all our teeth pulled out than admit it. There are a few of us who go bulldozing our way through life thinking we're just about perfect, which is a pity, for then there's no room for improvement and we have nothing to look forward to.

There was a woman in the New Testament who felt

some of those things about herself. She might not have felt dumb or ugly, but she sure did feel insecure and "bad." One thing you can bet your life on, she didn't feel "just about perfect."

She wouldn't have won a popularity contest, either. In fact she wouldn't even have been a runner-up or an also-ran. In fact, her mailing address might have gone something like this:

MOST UNPOPULAR WOMAN IN TOWN
BACK STREET (WAY BACK)
SYCHAR, SAMARIA
(NO ZIP CODE)

She kept to herself (which was easy to do; nobody wanted to have anything to do with her), minded her business, and made no attempt to "get into a group."

Now "getting into the group" in these days means socials and swapping visits and outings and such. But in those days, for women, it meant going to the well outside the village at sundown to draw water! There they would meet and exchange all the village gossip and find out who just had a new baby and who wasn't getting along with whom and who had a new outfit and what color it was and which latest herbs were good for a facial or for soaking your feet or curing your cold. This might sound corny today, but in those day it was the only social life women had and it was what you might call a big deal.

And this poor unhappy woman didn't even join those gabfests, the only social life in town. She went to draw her water at *noon* and got home with it as quickly as she could, so she wouldn't have to run into anybody.

Such was her humdrum dreary life. And such it would have remained, one dreary day dragging into the next, except that one day, out of the blue, it took an unexpected smashing earthshaking turn and she was spun around, never to be the same.

She was on her daily errand of drawing water at noon when it happened.

"This is the last thing I expected!"

Whatever your life is—humdrum or exciting—sooner or later you're bound to meet God. You might meet Him early, through your parents, or later, through a friend or a teacher or something you're reading, or by looking at a bit of nature's beauty and wondering how it all came to be, and getting *curious* about it. But somehow you meet Him. It's as if He suddenly turns up in your path through life, and says, "Look at Me. I'm God. And I'm for *real*." And it almost always comes unexpectedly, this smashing realization and recognition. Life just seems to suddenly take a surprising turn, and He is there, and He cannot be ignored; He's to be reckoned with.

The woman picked her way along the stony path toward the well, her empty water jug on her head. It was a half-mile trek to the south, and it was in the heat of the day.

The well was a famous one; it was known as Jacob's well, for it was near the land where Jacob[1] had built an altar and called it "God, the God of Israel." Later Jacob bought the land and gave it to his favorite son Joseph. And still later, Joseph, after a long reign in Egypt, had been brought back and buried there. The place was steeped in religious history and was very important to the Jews.

Well it was important to the Samaritans too, she thought, and she was a Samaritan and proud of it. It was hotter than usual, she thought. The well was in sight at last, she thought. And then she saw the stranger.

It was a Man, a lone figure sitting by the side of the well.

[1]In the Old Testament.

Resting perhaps, or waiting for someone. She didn't care. She was only glad it wasn't one of the women from the village—

Good grief. He was a *Jew.*

What in the name of common sense was He doing in Samaria? The Jews and Samaritans had been bitter enemies for hundreds of years. A Jew would trek miles out of his way to get wherever he was going rather than to go through Samaria.

Well at any rate, she wouldn't have to talk to Him.

A Jew would hardly speak to a *Jewish* woman unless others were around. A Jew speaking to a Samaritan woman? Yaaauk.

Well He was right in her path and it didn't look as if He were about to budge. She would just go around Him, do her job, and be on her way. She stopped and lifted her water jug off her head.

"Would you please give Me a drink?"

It was the Stranger! *Speaking* to her? Speaking to her.

She stopped in her tracks.

"What?" she said, astonished, "you—a Jew—are asking *me* for a drink? A *Samaritan* woman?"

They stood face-to-face. And she did not know it, but her life was about to take a surprising turn.

If you only KNEW

Do you think everything in your life happens by chance? Do you think *anything* does? Charles Spurgeon wandered into a prayer meeting one winter night. A blizzard was howling outside. He was practically the only one there. Young Spurgeon and the preacher. But that night, young Spurgeon met God. He stumbled back out into the blizzard, a changed lad. And he got to be the most powerful scholar and preacher of his generation, in England. Do you think it was a coincidence he met that particular preacher at that particular time? God stepped into his path, and Spurgeon looked up and *saw*.

Remember the story of the muckraker?[2] A shining being was standing in front of him, offering him a crown, but he was too busy raking muck to look up and see it. If he only knew . . .

Do you think it was a coincidence that the Samaritan woman went to the well at exactly that moment? If she'd been a few minutes earlier, she'd have missed the Stranger.

They stood face-to-face for a moment. And then the stranger said, "If you only knew what a wonderful gift God has for you, and who I am, you would ask Me for some *living* water!"

Living water?

"I can't believe what I can't see"

"You're talking about God, but I'm sitting *here*, loaded down with my problems. And I've got to find my own way out. What can *God* do for me?"

It's an easy question to ask; sometimes your problems can be very big and very real. And the problems for young people today are bigger than they've ever been before.

There's the story about an old couple asleep one night, and the old man suddenly awoke; he was sure he'd heard the old grandfather clock strike thirteen. *Thirteen?* He shook his wife. "Wake up, wake up," he whispered. "It's later than it's ever been before!"

So it is with you. It *is* later than it's ever been before. In the book, *The Cross and the Switchblade*,[3] the "gang-kids" in New York were faced with problems big enough to shiver your timbers. One of them was dope. And some

[2]Chapter 3.

[3]Wilkerson, David, "The Cross and the Switchblade," (New York: Pyramid Books, 1963).

of those kids were eleven years old. And their story could be told almost anywhere today—yes, your problems *are* bigger than they've ever been before.

So it was with the woman at the well. There she stood, loaded down with her problems, and this mysterious Stranger was talking to her about "the wonderful gift of God"—and that she should ask for "living water." Outrageous!

"But is God big enough for my problem?"

"But I can't see how *He* will do it. I have my own intelligence and my own know-how. It seems as if I could work it out better myself."

It seems a reasonable argument. For after all, you know your own capabilities and what you have to work with, and you just naturally want to work out your problems by using things you *know* about.

The woman thought so too. "Living water?" she said. "And how can You give me this living water? You don't even have a bucket to draw with, and the well is deep. I have my own water jug to let down. Why, I'm better equipped than You to give myself a drink. And are You greater than our ancestor Jacob who gave us this well? Why, we've been doing things this way for years!"

"Can't I bungle through by myself?"

Sure you can. And you'll even get some of your problems solved, on your own. But they'll keep coming back, with different clothes on. And one big basic problem will always be there. A sneaking feeling that there *is* something bigger, something greater, that you've somehow missed getting ahold of. And you have a built-in longing for it, even though you can't quite grasp what it is. You have a built-in longing for God. And you can't shake it; He put it there.

66

So bungle through if you must, but those pesky problems keep coming *back*.

The Stranger at the well looked at the woman. "Anyone who drinks this water will be thirsty again," He said, "but whoever drinks the water *I* give him will never be thirsty again. The water *I* give will be like a spring inside him, watering him forever with eternal life."

"Oh NOW I get it!"

" 'For God so loved the world that He gave His only begotten Son.' God loved me and gave His Son to die for me. And Jesus rose again. Now if I just accept this gift, accept Him as my Saviour, all my problems will disappear and my father will double my allowance and I'll start getting good grades without half trying and all my temptations will go away and life will be a snap."

There was an old man, way back in the mountains somewhere, and he was very poor.[4] He went to a revival meeting, heard what God had done for him, and accepted Jesus Christ. Then he immediately got down on his knees and said, "God, send me a barrel of flour and a barrel of sugar and a barrel of pepper . . ." Then he corrected the order. "No, God, wait a minute—that's too much pepper." And he went on with his list. He'd accepted Christ alright. But he'd missed the point. He thought God was Santa Claus.

Sound dumb? Think a minute. Without putting it in those words, we do the same thing. We just do it in more subtle ways.

The woman at the well was no different. "Never thirst again?" she said. "Please sir, give me some of this water! Then I'll never be thirsty again and I won't have to make this weary trek to the well every day."

[4]This is a true story.

Sound dumb? Well she didn't get the point either.

"Does God know all about me?"

Well we like to think He knows all the good things. But the bad ones! We'd like to hide them. Like Rachel in the Old Testament[5] hid her idols when her father walked into her tent. She just shoved them under a pillow and sat on them.

The Stranger at the well did not answer the woman's question. Instead, He said, "Go get your husband."

Ouch. This was a sore point. And she didn't want to talk about it. "I have no husband," she said.

"You never spoke a truer word," the Stranger said. "You have no husband *now*. But you *have* had five husbands. And you're not behaving yourself very well right now."

Ouch. There go all your faults, sliding out from under the pillow, all over everything.

The woman was flabbergasted. The Stranger knew all about her! He must be a prophet.

"You do it your way—I'll do it mine"

When you hear that Christ died and rose again for you, so you could face a holy God—that's good news. But when you're asked to admit that you're a sinner before you can accept that wonderful gift—*ouch.* That's when you try to squirm out of it. You put up an argument. You change the subject. There are all sorts of tricks. "Why is it," you say, "that there are so many denominations? And some people worship one way and some worship another and some people get sprinkled for baptism and some people immersed in water and some people take communion in their seats and

[5]Genesis 31:34.

some people go to the altar andsomepeopleare"dedicated" andsomepeopleare"confirmed"andsomepeople—"

It all comes tumbling out. Now you've got 'em! Let 'em give you an answer to *that.*

The woman tried the same thing. "Why is it," she said, "that the Jews insist Jerusalem is the only place to worship their way and the Samaritans say right here at Mt. Gerizim is the only place to worship *their* way and why is it—"

But the Stranger brought her right back to the point. "It's not *where* we worship,"[6] he said. The point is—is our worship *spiritual* and *real?* Do we have the *Holy Spirit's* help? For God is a Spirit and we must have the Holy Spirit's help to worship as we should. The Father wants *this* kind of worship from us.[7]

Yes. God is greater than any denomination.

"Got it. Now I'll put it away for the future"

"I grasp the whole point now. But I'm not ready for it yet." This the way you feel? And God still seems far away in the future?

Dwight Moody, the greatest evangelist of his generation, felt like that when he first went to Sunday School. His one ambition was to grow up and make a lot of money. He decided to put the whole idea away until he was old. Then one day his Sunday School teacher came into the shoe store where he was working, and told him that Christ died for *him,* and loved *him,* and wanted his love right *then.* And Moody accepted Christ *right then.* He was never the same again.

The woman? She tried putting it off too. "Well I know that someday the Messiah will come—the one they

---

[6]Or **how** we go through our rituals.

[7]Read John 4:22, 23, LNT.

call Christ—and when He does, He'll explain everything." There was plenty of time, she was saying; she'd wait till then.

And the Stranger said quietly, "*I* am the Messiah."

God was there, in her path, not sometime in the dim future, but *right then.*

Right NOW!

"Now is the time of salvation!" Paul wrote in his letters. "Believe on the Lord Jesus Christ!" he thundered to the Philippian jailor. And he meant "Right *now!*"

You didn't "just happen" to get to the right place at the right time and meet the right person or read the right book or hear the right lesson—in order to hear the gospel. God planned it! And He's standing in your path *right now.* And He's saying, "Look at Me. I am God. And I am for real."

What? You already know Him? And you have a problem? Give it to Him—*right now!*

The woman didn't "just happen" to meet Jesus that hot afternoon. He went through Samaria (where Jews never went) on His way to Galilee and stayed there by the well while His disciples went off to buy food and was waiting there when the woman came along *because He planned it.*

And the woman? Well, when the light finally dawned on her that she was face-to-face with Christ, she flew into action with "Right now!" ringing in her ears. She dashed back to her village in such a hurry that she left her water jug behind. She left her water jug—and her salvation—and her problems—in His hands.

And on with it!

Don't stop there. Get going!

The woman turned her village upside down. "Come see!"

70

she cried. "Come meet a man who told me everything I ever did! Can this be the Messiah?"

And when they saw her face ablaze with enthusiasm, they came a-running to see for themselves. And they listened to Jesus and begged Him to stay and tell them more. He did—for two days—and when He left, they said, "He is indeed the Saviour of the world."

"What can I do?"

Well you can read the story in John 4:1–42, for a starter. It's long, but it's so interesting you won't want to miss a verse. And you can memorize: "That if thou shalt confess with thy mouth the Lord Jesus, and shalt believe in thine heart that God hath raised him from the dead, thou shalt be saved."[8] And then you can—

Get going!

[8]Romans 10:9.

CHAPTER 7

"I Met the Most Wonderful Person Today!"

"Dear Diary: Whahoooo! And Woooeeee! I met the most *wonderful* person today! And it wasn't just casual either—this person offered me *friendship*. Did I want it? Boy, did I ever *want* it! It seems almost too good to be true—"

Do you keep a diary? What? And if you're a boy, do you think only silly girls keep diaries? Nonsense! Some of the most famous men in history (men of letters, statesmen, kings—yes, and even great generals) kept diaries. And we know a great deal more about history and letters today because those diaries have been dug out of moldy corners and pounced upon by scholars.

And if you ever found a diary and read: "I met the most *wonderful* person today—," you'd sure read on!

There was a girl, once, who kept a diary, and it was no nonsense. She was a beautiful airline stewardess, and her name was Carlie Lane.[1] One night her diary took a very important turn—in fact it became so important that before too many pages, it turned out to be a book, a *published* book —and Carlie became an author.

The night that diary took that sudden turn and became so important, was the night *she* met "the most wonderful Person." And the entry at the top of the page? It started with four simple words: "I accepted Christ tonight."

That entry changed her life.

Felipe Alou, veteran major league baseball player, may or may not keep a diary. But if he does—a life-changing entry might be back in one of those pages. For after his first game with the Giants, he got back to his hotel room to find a telegram from an old friend back in the Dominican Republic. "Congratulations, old friend," it went, "I have prayed for your success. But remember, even a big league ballplayer needs Christ. You'll find that baseball is not everything. 'Be not wise in thine own eyes: fear the Lord.'" Felipe's eyes brimmed with tears as he realized the telegram must have cost his friend half a week's wages. And he began to read the Bible *this very friend* had given him at the airport two and a half years before.[2]

The life-changing entry in his diary would be very much the same: "I accepted Christ today."

[1]Lane, Carlie, "I Walk a Joyful Road," Campus Life, January, 1968, pp. 17, 18.

[2]Hefley, Jim, "The Bravest Brave," Campus Life, April, 1966, p. 21 (adapted).

"But I'm not important like those people"

"They were terrific and exciting to begin with. And I'm full of sins and problems and everything."

Well it's the most life-changing event in your life whether you feel exciting or terrific or not.

There was a man from Gadara who—

Gadara? Oh it's a little town by the Sea of Galilee. And this man was not "terrific" either. He spent his days and nights wandering among the tombs and in the hills screaming and slashing himself with stones. When they shackled him with handcuffs and ankle straps he would snap them loose and be off again before they could catch him. What was wrong with him? We don't know; the Bible tells us he was possessed by demons. And that term covered a multitude of physical and mental diseases—and sin, in those days. At any rate, he not only was "not terrific"—he was a mess.

But one day his whole life was changed. What happened? Our Lord stopped off at Gadara and met this man and spoke to the demons and cast them out. And in a twinkling, this man was perfectly well. If he'd kept a diary, the entry that day would have been: "I met the most wonderful Person today!"

And then there was this woman from Magdala who—

Magdala? Oh it's a little town on the Sea of Galilee, just across from Gadara. In the Bible this woman is called "Mary Magdala" and "Mary Magdalene" and no one knows her real last name but it doesn't seem to matter what *it* was—it just matters who *she* was and what happened to her.

And who was she? She was a woman possessed by demons too. Now exactly how this affected her—whether it was physical, mental, or moral—we do not know. It's a pretty good guess, though, that she was not exactly a "terrific" person—she, too, was a mess.

75

Nor do we know what led up to the exciting thing that happened to her.

Did it happen in her hometown? Did a friend take her to a neighboring village to follow the crowds? All we know is that somewhere, somehow, she met Jesus. He "cast out the demons"—and in a twinkling her life was changed. If Mary had kept a diary, the entry that night would have been: "I met the most wonderful Person today!"

NOW what?

Well, suppose you *did* meet a wonderful person and your diary went something like this:

SUNDAY: I met the most wonderful person today! And he offered me friendship. Boy, do I *want* it—

MONDAY: Got a note from my friend today. Didn't bother to read it.

TUESDAY: My friend wanted to help me with a problem today but I didn't want to bother talking about it.

WEDNESDAY: My friend asked me a favor but I was too busy.

THURSDAY: Had a chance to tell others about my friend today but I didn't think of it.

FRIDAY: My friend seems so distant. I wonder why?

SATURDAY: Didn't think of my friend all day.

SUNDAY: Had a chance to get some info on my new friend but didn't bother to listen.

WELL WOULDN'T *THAT* BE STUPID!

Well if you had an entry in your diary like: "I accepted Christ today," and then followed it with entries like: "Didn't bother to read my Bible today," and "Had a problem today but didn't bother to pray about it," and "Had a chance to do something for the Lord today, but skipped it—too busy" and "I could have learned more about the Lord today in Sunday School but didn't bother to listen"—

Wouldn't that be stupid too?

DO something!

After you've met this "wonderful Person" Jesus Christ, and accepted Him as your Saviour, if it's for real, it will just have to "bust out" somewhere. It won't stay hidden.

Lovely Carlie Lane's first entry was "I accepted Christ tonight." And the whole thing could have stopped right there, but Carlie's faith was for real. And a few entries later: "Tonight I went to visit a needy family in our congregation, with my few gifts . . . Nothing in the world could match the wonderful Christmas feeling I got in that house . . . My heart just felt as if it would burst when I walked down those steps and back to the car . . . I am grateful to God for his wonderful gift to me."[3]

And with Felipe Alou, a few entries later, it would have been: "Talked with the guys in the locker room today." For Felipe Alou is famous for his "bull sessions" about the Lord in the locker room. Many a big leaguer has come to know Christ because of him. Felipe's "thing" is witnessing.

These people *did* something!

"But with me it's different"

"They're famous and they've got more to go on than I have. I have nothing to buck me up. Besides, nothing I do seems to *count*."

Well let's get back to Mary Magdalene.

Her diary entries would have been filled with exciting and wonderful things Jesus was teaching and doing. And sprinkled through it all would be her thanks for the opportunities to give and do and serve. Jesus went on a tour of the villages of Galilee, and "some women went along, from whom He had cast out demons or whom He had healed."

[3]Lane, Carlie, "I Walk a Joyful Road," Campus Life, January, 1968, pp. 17, 18.

Mary is mentioned, ever so casually, along with "many others who were contributing from their private means to the support of Jesus and His disciples."[4] She gave her money and her service and her time.

Nothing you do seems to count?

Nothing Mary did seemed to count, either. There's no further record of her until two years later when Jesus' ministry on earth was ended and He stumbled through the streets of His beloved Jerusalem, and out to the hill of Calvary, where He was crucified.

It is at Calvary that we hear of Mary Magdalene again. And the entries in her diary for the next few days might have gone something like this:

Diary of an ordinary woman

FRIDAY: Late this morning, they took Him to Calvary and nailed Him to a cross. There were three of them on crosses there—two thieves—and my Lord. I stood in the crowd, huddled together with His mother Mary and the other women—and John. The disciples had all fled, but John had come back. The crowds were jeering at Jesus, mocking Him. The Jewish leaders cried, "He saved others; let him save himself, if he is the Messiah whom God has chosen!"[5] I thought of all He had done for me. *Why* hadn't He saved Himself? *Why?*

A terrible darkness came over the earth and we stood huddled in that darkness, sick with despair.

Once He looked down at His mother and John. "Woman, here is your son!" He said to Mary. And to John, "Here is

[4]Luke 8:2, 3, LNT.
[5]Luke 23:35, TEV.

78

your mother." John stood even closer to the weeping woman and she leaned against him. Jesus was thinking of His mother's care, even as He was facing death.

The darkness still hung over us. And at three o'clock this afternoon, Jesus cried out with a loud voice, "Father! In your hands I place my spirit!"[6] And with these words, He died. His words rung in the air. He had said *before* that no man could take His life, that He would lay it down of His own accord!

And then the earth began to tremble and shake and the crowd just seemed to crumble away, breaking up in all directions, fleeing, some beating their breasts, some in bewilderment, until only a few of us were left. I stayed there, along with some of His friends, and the other women. We watched as Joseph of Arimathea and Nicodemus[7] took his body down from the cross and wrapped it in a linen cloth. We followed as they took Him to a new tomb in Joseph's garden. And we watched from the distance as they rolled the huge stone over the entrance.[8]

Then we came back home to prepare spices and ointments to embalm Him. It was sundown before we finished; the Sabbath was upon us. We shall have to wait until Sunday morning.[9] It is late, but I cannot sleep.

This is the blackest day of my life.

SATURDAY: I cannot write anything tonight. Today was the longest day in the world. Oh yes. Yesterday, after He died, the captain of the Roman soldiers handling the execu-

---

[6]Luke 23:46, TEV.

[7]They were members of the Jewish high court; Joseph went to Pilate for permission.

[8]The "stone" was an enormous stone disk set in a trough so it could be rolled like a wheel.

[9]It was unlawful to touch a dead body on the Sabbath, which was Saturday (but it began at sundown Friday).

tion cried out, "Certainly, he was a good man!"[10] Yes. He was the most wonderful Person I ever met in my life.

But now He's dead. I shall never see Him again.

SUNDAY: My hand is still trembling; I can scarcely write!

We went to the tomb before dawn this morning—and the stone had been rolled aside and the tomb was empty! We were terrified—we ran to tell the disciples. We found Peter and John, and they rushed to the tomb in utter disbelief. They thought we were just babbling. I followed them back. They looked in the tomb and then went on back home in complete bewilderment. Where *was* He?

After they left, I went to the tomb and looked in for myself.

And there, inside, were two white-robed angels sitting at the head and the foot of the place where His body had been! And they actually spoke to me! They asked me why I was crying and I told them my Lord had been taken away and I didn't know where they had put Him. Then I turned around to find a man standing behind me. It was scarcely light and my eyes were blurred with tears and I thought perhaps he was a gardener. He asked me why I was crying and whom I was looking for. And I told him, "Sir, if you took Him away, tell me where you've put Him, and I'll go get Him." Then he said one word.

"Mary."

And I don't know whether I whispered it or shouted it. I said, "Master!" It was all I could say. It was the Lord!

I started toward Him but He cautioned me not to touch Him but to go tell the disciples. "Go tell My brothers," He said. "Tell them that I go back up to Him who is My Father and your Father—My God and your God."

I stumbled out of the garden, still blinded by tears, and ran to tell them. I wanted to stay in the garden.

---

[10]Luke 23:47, TEV.

80

All day long I've heard my name. "Mary." Never had my name sounded so beautiful to me as when He said it.

You met the most wonderful person?

And what did you do about it?

Mary met "THE most wonderful Person," and she followed Him and served Him, not only on the glad days, but through ups and downs and all the black places and when it got dull and when it got difficult and when it seemed impossible.

There is no record of Mary after that Resurrection Day. But there was no record of her for two years before the Resurrection, and she was right in there, pitching. So it's a pretty good guess that she became a member of that great secret organization too.

She must have signaled the sign of the fish, many times, or traced it in the sand with the toe of her sandal.

"But she was right there"

"She was right there with the Lord. And Carlie Lane is right there in the limelight, and Felipe too. They can witness where it's exciting."

What about the man from Gadara? He wanted to "get in on the action" too. He wanted to go along with the Lord. But the Lord told him to stay right where he was and tell everybody what had happened to him. He did, and the Bible tells us that people came and listened to him and *marveled* at what the Lord had done.

And what about Felipe Alou's friend? The one back in the Dominican Republic? Why he's as important in Felipe's ministry as Felipe himself!

It's where you are that you serve, right in your own little corner, where the Lord put you. And the most important book for your name to be written in is the Book of Life in heaven.

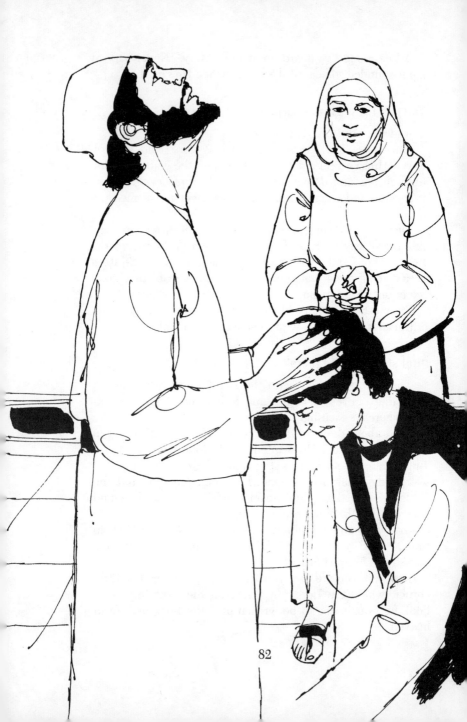

CHAPTER 8

"But I've Got All This Stuff Against Me"

"I'd like to really make it, you know, full steam ahead. Both in my life and for the Lord. But I've got all this stuff against me."

You'd like to really "make it?" Well there's no one pat formula, humanly speaking, that works exactly the same for everybody, for we're *individuals*, with different "bents." But for a starter, it's a pretty good idea to look at somebody who *did* make it, and find out what made him tick.

Take Timothy, for instance. Timothy was a young lad who lived in the area of Lystra and Derbe with his mother and father and grandmother. The great apostle Paul visited there, first with Barnabas, then with Silas,[1] and Timothy heard the gospel. And he later got to be one of Paul's closest associates. He was in Paul's company almost constantly for years. He traveled widely, he is mentioned in the opening salutation of six of Paul's epistles—and there are two books in the Bible addressed to him! Why he—

"Oh don't give me somebody like *that.* This guy didn't have my problems. Why this guy had everything going *for* him. I *don't.* In the first place—"

"You see, I've got this crazy background"

Yes. So many of us have. "My parents are divorced." Or, "I'm from a one-parent home. Other kids have both parents." Or, "One of my parents is a Christian and the other one isn't. There isn't any *unity* in our family." Or, "My parents are from different races. I feel sort of 'half-and-half.'"

Well, Timothy's mother and grandmother were Christians. But his father probably wasn't. And Timothy's mother was a Jewess. But his father was a Greek. The Bible tells us that *she had become convinced* (Timothy's mother, that is) "that Jesus is the Messiah, and the Author of eternal salvation, and yielded obedience to Him; but (his) [Timothy's] father was a Greek."[2]

This, to be vulgar, "knocks down" your first argument. And don't say, "But I'm young." So was Timothy.

[1]You can read this thrilling story in "The People Who Couldn't Be Stopped," a Regal Venture Book.

[2]Acts 16:1, Amplified.

"But I hate to study"

There's a letter in "Children's Letters to God"[3] that says:

Dear God: I would like to know what everybody is thinking. Is it possible?

Nope.

That kid, whoever he was, was dreaming. He wanted things the easy way, without trying to figure anything out for himself. He wished he had all the answers to everything, too, without digging for himself.

"If I'm going to be on the ball for the Lord I have to study. And I just hate to. I leave it all for Saturday night, to study my Sunday School lesson. And it just won't *jell.*"

Well, don't be ashamed of it. Most of us hate to study. The idea is, to make it painless—don't "goof off," and then "cram." It doesn't work. Big doses of study just make you sick to your stomach.

Psychologists tell us[4]

(1) Don't study for more than a half hour at a time. Then rest. Then study again. Study—rest—study. And study your "weakest" subject first! (2) Study at the same time and in the same place each night. And turn the radio and TV off! The work will get done that much faster. (3) Use, don't waste, the time you're in school (in your case, in Sunday School). It'll mean much less studying to do at home. Don't just dream the time away. (4) Take good notes in class; then all you'll have to do at home is review, not learn all over. (Okay—in Sunday School, *listen.*) (5) Ask questions in class. Don't take your confusion home with you, or studying will be a waste and a botch. (6) Start reviewing a week before a test. Don't wait till the last minute and *cram.*

---

[3] Los Angeles Times.

[4] "Resolved: Study Less, Learn More," Los Angeles Times.

In other words: Listen, think, do a little each day, and *don't wait till the last minute to cram!*

You hate to study? Well then, you're doing it the hard way. *It can be easy! And fun!* You'll be *amazed* at what a "little" each day can do for you!

Two years passed before Paul came back to Timothy's area, and Paul asked Timothy to "join his team."

Did Timothy suddenly start to "cram"?

Nope.

He already had it, and was practicing it, for the Bible tells us that "All the brothers in Lystra and Iconium spoke well of Timothy."[5]

He already *had* it—in his head and in his heart. He'd got it from his mother and his grandmother, in *spite* of the fact that his father probably wasn't a Christian.

He'd been "studying"—a bit each day.

It was a cinch.

Paul invited Timothy to join him and Silas. And before Timothy left to join them, a special ordination service was held. Timothy was ordained and given the authority of a minister of the gospel.[6]

"Wait a minute—I'm timid"

"I hate to face people. And when people give me a hard time I'm thrown. And I discourage easily. Besides, now that Timothy was a minister, people would just naturally listen to him. He didn't have problems any more."

He didn't? Wrong. He *did.*

The die-hard religious leaders did not believe that Jesus was the Messiah. And those who did, thought that you had to be a Jew to accept Him. They reared up on their hind legs and fought Paul and his team in every town. And

[5]Acts 16:2, TEV.
[6]See II Timothy 1:6.

sometimes followed him to the next town to start trouble there (they followed him from Thessalonica to Beroea, and he had to be hustled out of town to save his life). Timothy was along while these things were going on, and he suffered the same problems Paul did.

And timid? Why, when Paul sent him off on a mission to Corinth, he (Paul) sent a letter ahead and part of it went like this: "When Timothy arrives, look to it that [you put him at ease, so that] he may be fearless among you, for he is [devotedly] doing the Lord's work, just as I am."[7]

In Bunyan's *Pilgrim's Progress*, Christian[8] was going up the Hill of Difficulty. The going was rough, but he stuck at it, for at the top of that Hill was the Palace Beautiful, a place well worth visiting.

Well, this poor timid chap got to the top of the Hill, and there was the Palace all right, off in the distance, and more beautiful than he'd even imagined. But in front of the gates, on either side, were two dreadful lions, snarling and slobbering and acting as if they hadn't had a good meal in months. The Gatekeeper was shouting something, but Christian couldn't hear, the lions were roaring so. "I'm afraid to come," he yelled back at the Gatekeeper, "and I can't hear what you say—those lions!"

"Don't be afraid!" shouted the Gatekeeper, but the rest of what he said was lost in the roar. Christian was about to give up when he finally heard what the chap was shouting. "Those lions," he yelled, "won't hurt you! They're *chained!* And besides, they don't have any *teeth!*"

Pilgrim went sheepishly toward the Palace Beautiful. Those crazy lions might roar but they couldn't bite. All they could do was slobber.

Humiliating.

[7]I Corinthians 16:10, Amplified.

[8]The hero of the story.

Your problems are like those lions, when God is with you. The Bible tells us: "For the Spirit that God has given us does not make us timid; instead, his Spirit fills us with power and love and self-control."[9]

"But all I seem to do is fail"

"Nothing I try *works*. I bungle everything."

Well you're at the end of a long line of bunglers. You *learn* by bungling. There's a child's letter to God that goes:

Dear God: How do little kids always know that crawling comes first?

Marcy

Which makes the "little kids" smarter than we are, sometimes. They know that they have to learn by failing, and picking themselves up again.

Timothy failed. Yes, he did. Paul sent him to the church at Corinth to take care of a problem there. But the problem was more than Timothy could handle. An older, more experienced man[10] had to be sent in to take care of it. Timothy was still "crawling." But did he quit? Never! He was with Paul to the very end of his life! And was Paul discouraged with him? Never! He told Timothy, "Let no man despise thy youth."

In a comic strip, one character said to another: "Y'know what you are, don't you? You're a FAILURE!" And the other chap yelled back, "A failure? How *can* I be? I've never even TRIED!"

Right. If you never try, you'll never be a failure. But you'll never be much of anything else, either.

[9] II Timothy 1:7, TEV.

[10] Titus.

"Well I did try but I didn't get to be important"

"I'd like to be a leader, and I'm trying, but I always seem to get stuck with the humdrum things. I turn out to be an errand boy."

Well so did Timothy, or so he must have thought many times. To catch up with his "errands" you'd need a computer. First he went to Europe with the "team." Then he was left behind while Paul went on to Beroea. Then he was sent for. So it was Beroea next. Oooops, left behind again. Paul went on to Athens. Then poor Tim was sent back to Thessalonica. Then he was sent for again—this time it was Corinth. Next time we hear of him, he'd turned up in Ephesus. Then back to Macedonia, then to Corinth thento-TroasthenbacktoJerusalem—

Phew!

What was he doing? Well not just preaching and being in the limelight! He was delivering letters, acting as Paul's secretary, delivering money, delivering messages—delivering—

Go. Stay. Jump.[11] Wait. Take a letter. Go. Come. It was the story of Timothy's life!

So what are you going to do now?

All your arguments are knocked down.

"Yeah, but I still have one up my sleeve. Timothy was young, all right, but he was a *little* older than I am. I still have gobs of time."

A teacher wrote on a chalkboard once.[12] Just "25,550?" That's all. The kids were curious. "What's *that?*" they wanted to know. "That," said the teacher, "is the number of days a person lives if he reaches 70."

---

[11] And Timothy said, "How high?"

[12] Los Angeles Times.

89

The kids just stared at those numbers. Seventy *years* seemed like *forever*, but 25,550 *days?*

Good grief.

Well it's something to think about. Time's a-flying, even for *you.*

What? It should be 25,567? The teacher forgot the leap years?

Don't be fresh.

And how about memorizing what Paul told Timothy?

"Let no man despise thy youth; but be thou an example of the believers, in word, in conversation, in charity, in spirit, in faith, in purity."[13]

[13]I Timothy 4:12.

CHAPTER 9

Don't Look Now, but There's That Problem Again

"Everybody has problems? I thought I was all alone"

A group of young people had a bull session once. At first they were just talking, you know, rambling around. And then suddenly the discussion took a serious turn. They got talking about problems. And it turned out that they all had one thing in common. They *all* had 'em!

One was miserable because his parents (and teachers!) were too strict with him. Too much authority. And another was feeling lost and bewildered because his parents weren't strict *enough*—he felt they didn't care!

One confessed that he was secretly terrified of a bully at school. Another confessed he had an awful time making decisions. And another one—

So it went on, a regular truth session. And when they were through, they broke it up and all went home. Nothing got settled. For each one took his problem right along with him.

Try THIS problem on for size

You think you have problems? Well listen to the tale about the man who—

His name was Onesimus. He lived back in Colossae during the times of the early church. And he didn't have the problems Timothy had. This chap was a *slave*. An honest-to-goodness bought-and-paid-for slave. He wasn't even a person. He was *property*. True, he was the property of a Christian man named Philemon—but he was still *property*. In those days slavery was an accepted custom. Prisoners of war became slaves. And poor people who couldn't pay their debts became slaves of the lucky chaps they owed money to. People who stole and couldn't pay the fine became slaves of the men they'd stolen from. Slaves could be bought, sold, loaned, traded—

YOU: Well so can big league baseball players.
YOUR CONSCIENCE: Yes, but they get paid money for it, like hundreds of thousands of dollars. And they're still free. You're hedging. Read on:

And slaves were branded. In Egypt they were branded with fire, like cattle. Hebrews who were slaves because of debt could be released after six years, but if they wanted to remain with their masters[1] they had their ears pierced with

---

[1] What? Why would they choose to stay with their masters? Because they were treated a great deal better than slaves of Gentile masters. They often became like one of the family.

an awl. Sometimes they were tattooed with their master's name.

And if they ran away? It was the unpardonable sin! They might run all over the world to hide, but if anyone found them with that brand—[2]

Ship 'em back!

Like a motel key. It might travel all over the world in somebody's wallet, but it still belongs to that motel. "Drop this in the nearest mailbox" the key tag says. Slaves—with that dreadful brand—were about as safe. "Just drop him on the nearest caravan—with a guard."

Any old motel key that hankers to travel, doesn't stand a chance.

Slaves who hankered to travel, didn't either.

"You just turned me off"

"I don't want to hear about some guy who was worse off than I am. Right now I couldn't stand it. My problem is here and now and it's grinding me down and I don't *want* to face it." And if you tell me Onesimus bore it nobly I'll turn my hearing aid down."

News for you.

Problems have been with us since Adam and Eve. *All* of us. And they're here to stay. And no matter how unique your problem seems to be, basically *all* problems boil down to a few generalities. (1) You don't feel secure. (2) You don't feel loved and appreciated. (3) You don't have enough money (or personality or know-how, or whatever it is with you) to fulfill your "wants." (4) You are "left out of the group." (5) You aren't able to realize your goals. (6) You don't have enough freedom. (7) Your relationships are all wrong (you're angry with "them" or they're angry with

---

[2] That burned-in brand, that pierced ear, that tattoo, or whatever.

you). (8) You "never had a chance." And you could add a few more of your own.

Onesimus had every basic problem wrapped up in a package deal. And, no, he couldn't face his problems either. He ran away. Where did he get the money to travel? He "borrowed" some money from his master Philemon—enough to get him all the way to Rome. Well actually, he just plain outright *stole* the money and ran away to Rome, is what he did.[3]

He'd hoped to get lost in the crowds.

"It just so happened—"

"I really planned it *this* way, but it just so happened that—"

The lad in chapter 1 just started out to join the crowds, with his lunch packed—but it "just so happened" that he ran into Andrew and they got to talking and the next thing the lad knew, he'd come face-to-face with Christ, and the *next* thing he knew, his little lunch was feeding 5,000 people and he went on his way, never to be the same again.

You plan your days and you plan your life and you wallow in your problems and then "it just so happens that—"

And the strangest things *do* happen!

What? Coincidence?

Don't you believe it!

Nothing "just so happens." God is just two jumps ahead of you.

Well it "just so happened" that the apostle Paul[4] was in Rome, a prisoner to be sure, but allowed to live in a rented house with a guard. And Paul was preaching and

---

[3]And Onesimus' name meant "profitable" or "helpful." Nice going!

[4]Read the story in "The People Who Couldn't Be Stopped," A Regal Venture Book.

teaching about the Lord—how He had died and risen again—and how the early church had started and was going full blast—and how all these exciting things were happening and the church of Jesus Christ was spreading all over the world—

And what did Onesimus do?

He ran smack into Paul!

We don't know *how*. Whether he went to a meeting and heard Paul, or whether they just got to talking, or what. But he listened to the good news that Jesus is indeed the Son of God. And he just put his life into God's hands—and accepted this Christ, and became a Christian.

YOU: Wait a minute. Hadn't he heard it all before? His master Philemon was a Christian.

YOUR CONSCIENCE: Wait a minute. How many times did *you* hear it before it *dawned* on you?

YOU: Okay, okay. I'll read on.

Well anyhow, Onesimus became a Christian.

But.

It "just so happened" that Paul was a good friend of—

Philemon! Onesimus' old master!

Oh good grief.

"I've run smack into my problem again!"

Oh sure. God will "run you into your problem" again and again and again. Until you face it.

Onesimus had run into Paul and had become a Christian. But his problem was still there.

"But Lord, now that I'm a Christian—"

"Can't You just let all my problems go away? I'd like to think that all this joy, joy, joy they talk about means that my problems will just dissolve."

97

YOUR CONSCIENCE: Oh, come on, now. You wouldn't have any *steel* in your spine.

YOU: I'd like God to make everything all right so I could live happily ever after without having to go back and face stuff that's cluttering up my life—

CONSCIENCE: You wouldn't have any steel in your spine.

YOU: It would sure make things a lot easier, if my problems would dissolve.

CONSCIENCE: You wouldn't have any steel in your spine.

YOU: Who wants steel in his spine?

CONSCIENCE: (A BIG GLUM SILENCE.)

YOU: Okay. *I* do.

CONSCIENCE: I thought you'd never get the point. Read on:

"It's rough to go back and 'face it' "

It sure is. Because you're a Christian doesn't always mean it's *easy*. It does mean, though, that you're not facing it alone now; God is with you.

Well Onesimus went back. All the way back to Colossae, to face his master Philemon! Not that he wanted to. He'd become like a son to Paul, he'd been helping Paul, he felt important for the first time in his life.

But the minute he decided to go back, and face his problem, he found it wasn't the monster he'd thought it was. All the kinks in his life began to iron out!

Paul wrote a letter to Philemon—and what a letter it was! A good thing, too, for poor Onesimus was going back a runaway and a thief—he needed all the help he could get!

That very letter is none other than the book of Philemon in your Bible. Won't take you two minutes to read it—it's only 25 verses long. It's tucked away there, between "Titus" and "Hebrews." It's so short you'll miss it if you turn the pages too fast.

In this letter, Paul says to Philemon—"Philemon," he says —"Do me a favor . . . welcome my child Onesimus—I won him to the Lord,[5] here in Rome . . . welcome him as if he were *me* . . . how helpful he's been to me . . . if he has harmed you or stolen from you, charge it to me—I'll pay it back . . . once he was unprofitable to you, but now he is profitable to both of us . . ."

What a letter it is!

And what's more, Paul trusted Onesimus to go back to Colossae to deliver it—not under guard—but with another believer![6]

Onesimus must have spent the rest of his life in gratitude, living up to what his name really meant—"profitable." And it's a pretty good guess that he traced the "Secret Sign" many times, on walls, or with a stick in the sand . . .

What about you?

CONSCIENCE: What are you thinking?

YOU: I'm making up a list of all the possible *other* things I could do if I were Onesimus. Instead of going back and facing up to the problem. There must be an easier way out that's just as good. Like: (1) Drop my master Philemon a note and tell him I'm a Christian now and hope he'll forgive me. (2) Ask Paul to write to Philemon and explain that I've turned over a new leaf and I want to stay in Rome. (3) Forget about Philemon and hope he forgets about me. (4) Just pick myself up and go on and hope I'll never make *that* mistake again. (5) Forget about the whole mess and make believe it never happened. (6) Beg Paul not to tell on me. (7) Change to a new group of friends and start all over.

[5]That's why Paul called him his "child."

[6]Tychicus

CONSCIENCE: Well?
YOU: None of it will do.
CONSCIENCE: Then don't you have something to add?
YOU: Yup. (8) Go back and face it.

Your problems—and God

If you're a Christian, you'll still have problems—but you'll have the Lord to see you through. Paul knew this. Even while he was in prison, he could say, ". . . for I have learned to be satisfied with what I have. I know what it is to be in need, and what it is to have more than enough. I have learned this secret, so that anywhere, at any time, I am content, whether I am full or hungry, whether I have too much or too little." (Philippians 4:11,12,TEV.)

Onesimus had to learn it too.

And so do you.

102

CHAPTER 10

Men's Lives Fade Away—*But!*

The cat paused in his morning walk along one of the lower galleries of the Roman Colosseum and looked around at the majestic and decaying splendor. Below him, the center (its wooden floor long since gone) lay gaping open to reveal a confusion of tunnels and dressing rooms and cages—and a thousand ghosts. Above him were the gawking tourists. He looked at them with weary indifference (as cats will) and yawned insultingly at an eager camera. Then he settled himself in a box seat and, leaving the ghosts and the tourists to their own affairs, he washed his paws.

A few blocks away was the Circus Maximus—the gardens of Nero. Everything was in shambles over there too. Absolute ruins. The cat stretched and closed his eyes. He might take a walk over there later in the day. After sundown the tourists went away, and he'd have privacy, alone with the bats and the owls.

He stretched again. It wouldn't matter which place he spent the night—the Colosseum or the Circus Maximus. Either one was a good place to prowl. They were both deserted.

All mankind is like grass, and men's lives wither and fade away.

. . . . . .

The Colosseum and the Circus Maximus were not always like they are today. Once they were ablaze with excitement and on fire with the most outrageous sin. Especially during the days of Nero, when he was persecuting the Christians who had invaded the Roman Empire—

But the story begins farther back than that.

. . . . . .

The Christians "invaded" the Roman people long before they ever "invaded" Rome. Way back when Jesus was on earth, Romans who lived in His area were hearing the good news of God.

There was that Roman Centurion[1] in Capernaum who was so impressed with the things he'd heard about God, that he built a synagogue! And when his servant was dying, he sent some of his soldiers to Jesus, to ask for healing. But before Jesus arrived at his house, this Centurion sent friends to meet Him and to give Him the message—"Don't trouble yourself to come, for I'm not worthy to have you in

[1]A centurion is a Roman officer in charge of a hundred soldiers. Very important fellow!

my house. Just give the order and my servant will get well!"[2]

What faith!

And there was that Centurion at the cross. When the darkness came, and the earthquake, he cried out, "He really was the Son of God!"[3]

Then there was that Centurion in Caesarea. Chap by the name of Cornelius. He worshiped God, but he didn't know about Christ. And one day he was praying and an angel appeared to him and told him to send for Peter, who was in Joppa. He did. Would Peter come? Peter would.[4]
And *another* Roman Centurion (and his family) heard the gospel and accepted Christ.

And then there was Julius—that Centurion who was sent along to guard Paul, who saved Paul's life, and stayed with him while he was in Rome. He undoubtedly heard the gospel (nobody could be with Paul and *not* hear it).

And so Christianity spread to the Romans—and not only among the poor, but among the rich, and among the VIPs in the Roman army!

Why when Paul finally reached Rome, who should come to meet him as a welcoming committee—but a band of Christians!

They were already there. Rome had been "invaded."

And Rome was getting concerned.

These pesky Christians were getting so powerful there, that they could no longer be ignored.

Nero was Emperor of Rome. The storm clouds were gathering.

Nero! And what a villain *he* was! He'd killed his mother,

[2]You can read the whole story in Luke 7:1—10. Yes, the servant did get healed.

[3]Matthew 27:54, TEV.

[4]Peter had to get rapped on the knuckles first. Read the story in "The People Who Couldn't Be Stopped," A Regal Venture Book.

his brother, two of his wives, and any leader of Rome who got in his way. Today we name our sons Paul. We might name a *dog* Nero. But it would be a dirty trick to play on a dog. Or even a pet *rat*.

Anyhow, while Nero was emperor, one of the most famous and terrible catastrophies in history took place.

Fire!

It raged through Rome for seven days and six nights. And when the last flame had died down, nearly all of Rome was in smoldering ruins.

And then the rumors started to fly. Was the fire an accident? Was it deliberately set? And if it was—*who?*

Nero!

He'd started it so he could rebuild the city and call it Neropolis! Or so one of the rumors went.[5]

Well Nero was not about to take that lying down. He looked about for a scapegoat.[6]

Why of course! The pesky Christians!

They were cordially hated anyhow; they wouldn't participate in "community life"[7] —they seemed to be against the human race!

Get the Christians!

Nero got busy.

The Christians were hunted down and vast numbers of them were captured.

Make a sport of it!

They were covered with the skins of wild beasts and torn to pieces by dogs. They were tortured and killed in the giant Colosseum, a sport for all to see. And Nero had chariot races in his beautiful gardens—the Circus Maximus. And when darkness fell, he provided light by living

[5]No one ever **proved** anything; it's still a mystery today.

[6]Someone to blame it on.

[7]Most of which was pagan ceremonies.

torches. Christians were fastened to crosses, their clothes soaked with wax, and set on fire!

It was one of the worst persecutions in history.

And Nero?

His wickedness was so great and his private life so scandalous that in time, even his own government began to hate him.

He finally died, by his own hand.

.　.　.　.　.　.

All mankind is like grass, and men's lives wither and fade away . . .

.　.　.　.　.　.

The Secret Sign went on. The persecution did not wipe out Christianity—it only made it grow.

Christians met secretly, in homes, in the catacombs,[8] anywhere and everywhere. And they identified each other by the Secret Sign. It was scrawled on walls, written in the dirt, carved on the tombs in the catacombs—

The sign of the fish. "Jesus-Christ-God-Son-Saviour!

And Christianity grew—and grew—and *grew*—through more ups and downs than there is time to tell here. Until 300 years later—

The Emperor Constantine proclaimed Christianity the legal religion of the Roman Empire! And by now, the Roman Empire included all the countries of the Mediterranean world!

Christianity!

From its birth in an upper room in Jerusalem on that day of Pentecost—to this!

It is one of the most amazing facts of history.

---

[8]Caves beneath the ground, off the Appian Way. Miles and miles of them!

But the story wasn't over. Christianity continued to have ups and downs. For months. And years. And centuries.

. . . . . .

All mankind is like grass, and men's lives wither and fade away . . .

. . . . . .

Why did it grow? And why is it growing? *How come?*

Because Christians continued to risk their lives, yes, and lose them, to keep it growing.

There was Polycarp. He was a man who was a personal friend of the apostle John. And an important leader in the church in Smyrna. A bright light in the early church. He was arrested—and doomed to die. He asked for an hour to pray. And he prayed so earnestly that his guards were sorry they had any part in his arrest. Just before he was to be burned publicly, the governor gave him one more chance. "Deny Christ. Deny Christ, and you shall live." His answer? "Eighty-six years have I served him, and he never once wronged me. How then shall I blaspheme my King, Who has saved me?"

He died—burned at the stake.

And there was John Wycliffe. Who was John Wycliffe? Oh, he was the man who, centuries later, translated the Bible from the Latin into common English, so people could read it and understand it. And when *he* was brought before his persecutors, he cried out, "With whom do you think you're contending—with an old man on the brink of the grave? *No!* You're contending with the *Word of God!*"

And *years* after he was buried, the powers-that-be were still so mad at him, they dug up his bones—and burned them—and scattered the ashes in a brook. But those ashes, like his influence, went from the brook to the river to the sea—and to the ends of the earth!

To *you.*

And there was Elizabeth Welsh, wife of John Welsh; he'd been preaching the gospel all over England and France.[9]

He was exiled from his beloved Scotland and ordered never to return.

And when, toward the end of his life, his wife Elizabeth appeared before the godless king—

The king knew she was John Welsh's wife.

"And whose *daughter* are you?" he asked.

"John Knox's daughter, sire," she said.[10]

The king leaned forward. "Knox and Welsh!" he cried. "Surely, the devil never made such a match as this!"

And she came back with a dinger.

"Indeed he did not, sire," she said, "For we never asked his advice!"

Ha!

The king's court was in an uproar.

"And what, precisely, are you here to ask of me?" the king said.

"That my husband might be allowed to come back to his beloved Scotland and die in his native land."

Ah! Now! The king had the upper hand. Did she want her husband to come back?; And if she did—if she *really* did—

"Your husband may come back," he said—"on one condition. That he will bow down to my bishops."

"He bows down to no one but Christ."

"That he will bow down to my bishops!"

There was a great silence.

And then, Elizabeth Welsh, weighing under a hundred

---

[9]And what a story **that** is!

[10]John Knox **was another** chap who'd been preaching the gospel, but **good.** He'd upset all England!

pounds with rocks in her pockets, faced the great and powerful king.

And she raised her apron, and made it into a pocket, held before her.

"Please, sire," she said, "I'd rather have his head—right here." Right there in her apron.

There was another great silence.

And she walked out.

Well, John Welsh didn't wind up with his head in his wife's apron.

He died in his bed, a few weeks later, right after preaching to a great audience.

But Elizabeth Welsh had *risked her neck*.

For all she knew, they'd *both* be killed.

There were others. So many of them, that if their tales could be told, they would fill a library.

They marched, like a great army with banners, down through the ages—

They lived—and died.

And their persecutors lived—and died.

.　.　.　.　.　.

All mankind is like grass, and men's lives wither and fade away—

BUT THE WORD OF GOD GOES ON FOREVER!

.　.　.　.　.　.

The cat got up and stretched again. It had been a long nap. The tourists were gone. It wouldn't matter which place he spent the night—the Colosseum or the Circus Maximus. Either one was a good place to prowl.

They were both deserted. Except for the bats and the owls.

. . . . .

All mankind is like grass, and men's lives wither and fade away—
BUT THE WORD OF GOD GOES ON FOREVER!

. . . . .

YOUR CONSCIENCE: Well?
YOU: Well, what?
CONSCIENCE: The Word of God will go on, in *spite* of you. But how wonderful if it *does* go on BECAUSE OF YOU.
YOU: What can *I* do?
CONSCIENCE: You can spread the word, in your own little circle, in your own little way.
YOU: How? (And you can write this in yourself!)

. . . . .

For a starter, you might memorize this:
"For all flesh is as grass, and all the glory of man as the flower of grass. The grass withereth, and the flower thereof falleth away: But the word of the Lord endureth forever. And this is the word which by the gospel is preached unto YOU."[11]

[11]I Peter 1:24, 25.

CHAPTER 11

"I Don't Know the Way Out!"

"I have all these problems and stuff, and I don't think I did anything to deserve them—all I did was get *born*. And I grew and grew—and now, suddenly, my life is in shambles and I have all these questions—how did I ever *get* into such a mess? I didn't *ask* for it. And what *is* the way out?"

Good question.

And the way *out* is *in*.

Into eternal life, through Jesus Christ. And the way isn't *what*. It's *who*.

"Now WAIT a minute!"

"I *know* all this. And I know it sounds dumb, but I know all this and I still don't know exactly what it *means*. I know that Jesus died for me. Because, somehow, I'm a sinner.

"Well, I haven't murdered or anything. And how can I be as bad as a murderer is? I mean, I'm just a plain-vanilla *kid*. Exactly what *is* sin? And what *is* my way out?"

Another good question. And there's a good answer.

Let's go back to the very beginning.

In the beginning—

"In the beginning, God created the heavens and the earth." He flung out the sun and the moon and enough planets and galaxies of stars to boggle the imagination. He called it all the universe and it was vast beyond words to describe.

You know the story of creation well. But the point that concerns us here, is that God created *man*. And gave him a mind of his own. And gave him the privilege of making his own decisions!

And what did man do with this privilege?

He used it to disobey God!

You know that story well, too. God said, "Don't do it." And Satan said, "Do it!"

And man made up his own mind, and *did* it.

He disobeyed God.

And he thereby took himself right out of God's hands.

And *that's* what sin is. Being out of God's hands. For man could never be anything but sinful, all by himself, without a holy God.

And right then and there, God made a promise. It was as if He said, "Man has taken himself out of My hands, and he is lost. But I'll get him back again. For in due time[1] I shall send My only Son, and He shall die for the sin of man.

[1]When He was good and ready. And He wasn't in a hurry.

114

"He will be My gift to man.

"His name shall be called 'Jesus.'

"Then any time, down through the ages, any man or woman or boy or girl who wants to—*can make up his own mind,* and accept this gift, and put his life back into My hands again."

And that's what "being saved" is. Putting yourself *back into God's hands.*

It's as simple as that.

"If it's all so simple, what's the problem?"

"I mean, when God provided such a simple solution, why didn't man just take it? I mean, why did he have to go and botch it all up? Why didn't God just make man accept this gift and prevent all this trouble, down through the ages? It's why the world is in such a mess now!"

That's just the point. God doesn't *make* man do anything. He gave man the privilege of making his *own* decisions.

Now, who made the mess?[2]

"But when Jesus came—why didn't HE tell them?"

"Why didn't He just come right out and *tell* them what it was all about?"

He did.

He told them all over again, what the prophets of old had already told them.[3]

He told them all through His ministry, again and again and *again.*

He told them at the Feast of Tabernacles, a few months before His crucifixion. Right there in Jerusalem.

---

[2]Well, **think** about it.

[3]You can read what the prophet Isaiah had already told them in "Which Way to Nineveh?," a Regal Venture Book.

The Feast of Tabernacles? Well it was *the* feast of the year, held in the fall, when the crops were gathered in and it was a time of rejoicing, and thanksgiving to God. They brought in their offerings, and built booths, and celebrated. Celebrated the time when God had brought them out of Egypt. And gave them water from the rock, when Moses struck it. And guided them with a pillar of cloud by day, and a pillar of fire by night.

What did they do to celebrate the giving of the water? Well the priest brought water from the pool of Siloam to the Temple Hill in a golden pitcher. He poured the water on the altar in the Temple and the people chanted Psalm 118. And there was music—cymbals, trumpets—

It was very impressive.

But on the last day of the feast?

No water ceremony.

It was their way of saying they no longer needed it; God had provided it.

And what did Jesus do?

He gave them the shock of their lives!

He stood up, and in a loud voice, said, "If any man thirst, let him come unto ME, and drink!"[4]

And before they could recover, He went on— "AS THE SCRIPTURE SAYS, 'Whoever believes in ME, streams of living water will pour out from his heart!' "[5]

What could be plainer?

But they didn't believe Him.

And what did they do to celebrate the pillar of fire?

After the first day of the feast, and for the next seven days, they lighted tall candelabras in the Court of the Women. Each candelabrum had four bowls holding seven and a half gallons of oil. The wicks? Cast-off clothing of the

[4]John 7:37.

[5]John 7:38, TEV.

priests. The light? Shone all over Jerusalem! The celebration? Flaring torches![6] Music![7] Praises to God!

Impressive!

Yes.

But the next day[8] when Jesus went back to the Temple to teach, He told them all over *again*.

The candelabras were out. The light was gone.

The celebration of the Feast of Tabernacles was over. And what did He say?

"I am the light of the world: he that followeth ME shall not walk in darkness, but shall have the light of life!"[9]

You see, He *told* them.

But they didn't believe.

And what did He tell His disciples the night of the Last Supper?

"I am the Way—yes, and the Truth and the Life. NO ONE can get to the Father except by means of ME."[10]

But they didn't understand.

He told them and told them and *told* them.

HE TOLD EVERYBODY.

What could be *plainer?*

What's the way out?

The way out is the way *in*. The way into eternal life. And it begins, for you, right now, the moment you accept this gift.

[6]Men of high standing carried them.

[7]The instruments were played by Levites standing on the fifteen steps which led from the Court of Israel into the Court of the Women.

[8]He'd been up in the Mount of Olives all that night, praying.

[9]John 8:12.

[10]John 14:6, LNT.

"For if you tell others with your own mouth that Jesus Christ is your Lord, and believe in your own heart that God has raised Him from the dead, you will be saved. For it is by believing in his heart that a man becomes right with God; and with his mouth he tells others of his faith, confirming his salvation. For the Scriptures tell us that *no one who believes in Christ will ever be disappointed.*"[11]

And then you *live* it.

"Be ye therefore followers of God, as dear children; For ye were sometimes darkness, but now are ye light in the Lord: WALK as children of light."[12]

It's like one great Christian said, "If I had my life to live over, *I'd just believe God!*"[13]

God promised it at the very beginning.

Jesus told people, while He was on earth.

And the Bible is telling you, right now.

Why don't *you* believe Him?

Right now.

Jesus says to *you*—"*I* am the Way!"

[11]Romans 10:9–11, LNT.

[12]Ephesians 5:1, 8.

[13]Dr. Henrietta Mears.

120

CHAPTER 12

Get in There and *Win!!!*

"Yaaaaaaah!"

Whatever sport we're watching, we're apt to go all out and shout ourselves hoarse for our heroes. "Run with that ball! Make that basket! Get him *down!* Run! Run! Get in there and winnnnnn!"

Or if *we're* in the game, or the race, or the match, or whatever, we hear the spectators shouting for *us*. And though our muscles might be fairly bursting, we spur ourselves on, to do or die.

We play to win.

Sports have always been with us

This enthusiasm about sports is nothing new. Sports were with us back in Paul's time too. Only back then, you couldn't get out the peanuts and watch them on TV. You had to get to the arena!

From all over the empire, the people flocked to games and contests and races—

The amphitheaters built for them were tremendous, and the crowds were great enough to cause major traffic jams.

The athletes trained to within an inch of their lives, and watched their diets and had lists of "must-eats" and "no-nos" as long as your arm.

It was a life of discipline, but it paid off. It was—

Why it was amazingly like the Christian life!

Paul thought so too.

As he wrote his letters of instructions to Christians, it kept popping out, over and over again—this comparison of the Christian life with sports.

Christians couldn't fail to get it, for they were either sports fans or at least *knew* about sports.

So, without pulling his punches, Paul drove his points home.

Some of them hit where it hurt.

They still do today

"Oh my achin' muscles!"

Yes. Training *hurts*. But it's impossible to imagine being an athlete without it. And it's impossible to imagine being a *good* one without *plenty* of it.

Paavo Nurmi was one of the greatest track and field athletes in the sports world. Some of the nicknames they gave him sound like a TV super-hero. Peerless Paavo, the Ace of Abo, the Phantom Finn! He shattered every record in the books from 1,500 meters to 10,000 meters, from one mile up to six, up to one hour of running. Unconquered and all-conquering was ole Peerless, standing head and shoulders above all competitors.

Luck? Well, even as a boy, Paavo knew what he wanted to be. *He trained more than others,* the reports say. He developed his even pace by running behind trolley cars. He set himself a program that stressed speed, stamina, and condition. Luck? What do *you* think?

"But what about the guys who don't seem to have to work at it? The ones who are just naturally great?"

Well, take ole Morris Kirksey, now—there was a great one. Potentially, the greatest sprinter who ever lived. Poetry in motion. Great fighter, too. *Yet he never realized the future to which he was justly entitled.* For during the formative period of his muscles, he had no competition. He won his school races with ease, never stretching his tendons. Then later when the really strenuous competition came along, his muscles couldn't stand the strain They pulled. They tied up in knots. Ole Morris was still a great athlete— but the point is, he could have been greater if he'd trained harder.

Paul has a word to say to the Christian about training. "Every athlete in training submits to *strict discipline . . .*"[1]

"Keep yourself in training for a godly life. Physical exercise has some value in it, but spiritual exercise is valuable in EVERY way, for it promises life both for now and for the future."[2]

Are you for real?

Or are you a phony? Do you mean business—or are you just fooling around? You can't be the genuine article and a phony at the same time. If you're going to "play the game" —*you have to obey the rules.*

[1] Read I Corinthians 9:24.

[2] I Timothy 4:7, 8, TEV.

123

The athletes who got to the top—and *stayed* there—were the ones who obeyed the rules.

Take Bo McMillin for instance. Ole Bo was a star quarterback in grammar school. When he got to college, his famed running pass made his name a household word. He belonged to a team that was training for something big. And obeying the rules was important; Ole Bo would stand on a table in the locker room and yell, "If I see anybody break training rules I'm going to whip him then and there." And nobody did. They knew Ole Bo meant business. The college? Oh a little one-horse college in Danville, Kentucky. And what was the "something big" they were training for? Oh to beat Harvard, that's all. And what's more they *did* it And who was their key man? Ole Bo McMillin. "I'd rather be Bo McMillin today than governor of Kentucky," one man said. Who said it?

The governor of Kentucky.

Paul had a thing or two to say about obeying the rules. "An athlete," he wrote to Timothy, "can't win the prize he's after unless he obeys the rules!"[3] He might not have stood on a table in the locker room, but you can bet he must have said to Timothy more than once, "If I see you break the training rules I'm going to whip you then and there."

Or words to that effect.

"Who wants to look at me?"

One great thing about being an athlete is that in his moments of glory, there are always spectators to roar and cheer and make him feel like king-o'-the-mountain. He gets all his glory in public. Unfortunately, he makes all his mistakes in public too.

There are witnesses!

Take Joe Lewis. Ole Joe was king-o'-the-mountain, all

[3]Read II Timothy 2:5.

right. The great Brown Bomber, the Detroit Battler, the most interesting heavyweight in the world, superman who had everything—boxing ability, punching power—it was clear to all the world that he was the coming champ.

Until he met Max Schmeling.

He lost. Not by a hair By a knockout, in the twelfth round.

And there were witnesses. Plenty of them.

But actually this loss to Schmeling did more to make Ole Joe a great fighter than anything else in his career. He "grueled" for a comeback. And he got it. Two years and ten fights later, he met Schmeling again.

A knockout again. In two minutes, four seconds. Who got knocked out?

Schmeling.

And there were witnesses.

Paul says Christians have witnesses too "As for us, we have this large crowd of witnesses around us. Let us rid ourselves, then, of everything that gets in the way, and the sin which holds on to us so tightly, and let us run with determination the race that lies before us."[4]

Paul is saying something else here, too. Did you notice? Get rid of all the stuff that gets in the way! With Christians, the "stuff" is sin. Get rid of it!

Athletes get rid of all excess clothing that clings, *anything* that "gets in the way."

Even long hair, with track runners, is out. Too much wind resistance.

And you can bet that Ole Joe "got rid of" anything that got in his way when he was training for that comeback.

"Sometimes it's a real tussle!"

Yes, sometimes it is. And Paul knew it, too. He even

[4]Hebrews 12:1, TEV.

compared it with a good knock-down-drag-'em-out-fight!

Now Ole Joe was boxing with Schmeling. And if you're a girl, reading this, why quite naturally you won't box or wrestle. (There *are* lady wrestlers, but who wants to *be* one?)

So what's it to you?

Well Paul says we are wrestling with *sin.* Ever have a sin come into your life? And you win by a knockout? And then you *lose* by a knockout? And you gruel for a comeback?

You're wrestling with sin.

Paul says, ". . . build up your strength in union with the Lord, and by means of his mighty power. . . . for we are not fighting against human beings, but against the wicked spiritual forces in the heavenly world, the rulers, authorities, and cosmic powers of this dark age."[5]

Your greatest opponent is *Satan.*

Get in there and win!

"But I keep losing bouts!"

Of course you're going to lose a bout now and then. You're not perfect *yet.* We have this tendency to keep our little failures all tucked away, like relics in a trunk. And we just love to get them out and fondle them, feeling oh-so-sorry for ourselves.

Well, don't.

There was a lad, once, who couldn't play *any* sport well. When he went to play baseball, he couldn't hit. When he went to play basketball, he couldn't dribble. And if he picked up a dart, people started running. Somehow he bumbled into football. When he finally made the Los Angeles Rams, he did one thing consistently. He got started and yanked and started and yanked and started and yanked—

[5]Ephesians 6:10–12, TEV.

126

But he didn't quit.

And what and who is he today?

Why he's *Dr.* Frank Ryan who was the "scholar" quarterback of the Cleveland Browns, and one of their most valuable players.

Oh yes. While he was bumbling his way through life, he managed to earn a Ph.D. in math at Rice Institute.

"If at first you don't succeed," he says with a grin, "fail, fail again."

So put your past failures in the trunk and close the lid and sit on it. Just pick yourself up and go on with the game.

"Don't quit!" Paul says: "Let's not get TIRED of doing what is right, for after a while we will reap a harvest of blessing if we don't get discouraged AND GIVE UP"[6].

"But some of my failures aren't really my *fault*. I just have all these troubles getting in my way."

Well, don't keep your eye on your troubles either. Paul says, "Let us keep our eyes fixed on JESUS, on whom our faith depends from beginning to end. He did not give up because of the cross!"[7]

Hold it, HOLD it!

Don't go overboard. Past failures are one thing—present "weak points" are quite another. Own up to your weak points, and see them for the culprits they are. Where do you fall down? What's holding back your progress? Well don't ignore it. It probably won't go away.

Know Willie Mays? He's the chap who put the Giants on the map. "Listen," any Giants fan will tell you, "Willie can throw and hit and catch and run better than anyone who

[6]Galatians 6:9, LNT.

[7]Hebrews 12:2, TEV.

ever lived and he's the guy who's gonna break Babe Ruth's record."

Yes. Ole Willie could do all of these things. But in running, he had one little weak point

He kept running into fences.

He got to running and just—couldn't—stop.

This, clearly, got Ole Willie into a lot of trouble.

"What about running into fences?" a sportswriter asked him once.

"Well," said Ole Willie, "I practice. I practice *not* running into fences. First coupla weeks of training, I go out to the outfield and run at the fences fast as I can. Then I stop. That way, I get used to running near the fences, know what I mean, but I get used to stopping just in time."

Ole Willie knew his weak points. And he practiced strengthening them.

Good idea for the Christian. Know your weak points. And practice strengthening them.

Now Ole Willie could have just refused to recognize his weak point, and gone on smashing into fences. But he knew better.

He is a real champ.

"But I already know it all!"

"I'm stuffed with knowledge up to my eyeballs! I know my Bible and I know all the verses and I study my lesson and I'm first with my hand up for answers and—"

Great. But if you're not putting it into practice—watch it!

Remember Ole Doc Ryan? The "scholar" quarterback of the Cleveland Browns?

Had an I.Q. of 155.

Smart guy

"But he used to over-think himself," said his coach, Blanton Collier.

And Ole Doc Ryan agreed.

"I'd get so wrapped up in strategy that when I got to the line of scrimmage I couldn't switch it into the *mechanics*. I'd study the films. And I'd concentrate. But I couldn't put what I'd learned into practice. I had a hard time switching. The process of becoming a skilled quarterback is—well, you've got to be thrown into the fray and live or die in it. It's a process of learning, and the *only way you can learn is to be out there, under game conditions. You have to PLAY.*"

That's the whole idea.

You can be "stuffed with Bible knowledge up to your eyeballs." But the only way to really learn is to get out there and *live* it.

And get out there to win!

"What's in it for me?"

Well, the reward for the "athletes" in Paul's day was a crown of leaves—olive, pine, laurel—even parsley

What would happen to it? It would dry up, of course. But was it ever held in high honor!

But the crown for the Christian *does* last.

"Every athlete," says Paul, "submits to strict discipline; he does so in order to be crowned with a wreath that will not last; but we do it for one that will last forever."[8]

And in his letter to Timothy, Paul says:

"As for me, the hour has come for me to be sacrificed; the time is here for me to leave this life. I have done my best in the race, I have run the full distance, I have kept the faith. And now the prize of victory is waiting for me, the crown of righteousness which the Lord, the righteous Judge, will give me on that Day—and not only to me, but to all those who wait with love for him to appear."[9]

[8]Read I Corinthians 9:24–27.

[9]II Timothy 4:6–8, TEV.

But the most *startling* thing in this business of crowns, for the Christian, is written in the very last book of the Bible:

"I am coming soon. Keep safe what you have, so that no one will rob you of your victory prize!"[10]

Which brings us right back to *you*.

Don't ever think you've arrived

Doing very well, are you?

Good.

But you can be better.

Just don't ever think you've "arrived."

Take Ralph Beard. Ole Ralph was all-American, voted outstanding basketball player in the nation, at one time. And what did he say to his coach? "Well," says his coach, Adolph Rupp,[11] "on the way home from the game with Utah, he came to me and wanted to know what he could do to improve his game. Here was *the most valuable player in the nation* asking for *advice*. Which only goes to show the qualities that make him such an outstanding athlete."

Ole Ralph was the "greatest."

But he was still looking for ways to improve.

So it should be for you.

Keep *safe* what you have, so that no one will rob you of your victory prize!

The crown is for real. The crown is for keeps.

Get in there—and *win!*

[10]Revelation 3:11, TEV.

[11]You think **your** name is funny?

130

CHAPTER 13

You Can Ignore It—
but It Won't Go Away!

A pop newspaper printed a real weird edition once. All the bad news was left out! Honestly! All war news, all strife, all crime, all smears, all hate—every last smidgeon of anything that might be disturbing, was gone!

And where the bad news might have been—only gaping empty spaces!

And somehow those empty spaces looked strangely *scarey*.

For any reader with an ounce of sense knew that ignoring the bad news *did not make it go away*.

Supposing the Bible were printed with all the bad news left out. No sin, no battles, no Satan, no—

132

But wouldn't those big empty spaces look strangely *scarey?* For you'd know that ignoring the bad news would not make it go away.

Now.

Supposing the Bible were printed with all the *good* news left out?

God's promise of a Saviour, His sending a Saviour, Jesus' promises—that He would die, that He would rise again, that He would be taken back up into heaven, that He was coming again—

That He is coming again!

Would empty spaces make it not so?

Would ignoring God's promises make them go away?

No.

Ignoring *bad* news won't make it go away. Ignoring *good* news won't make it go away either.

You feel like a "What's-his-name?" A reject? You've got "all this stuff" against you? There's that problem again? You don't know the way out?

Get in there and *win!*

For He said, "Then the Son of Man will appear, coming in the clouds with great power and glory." (Mark 13:26, TEV.)

And He said, "And if I go and prepare a place for you, I will come again, and receive you unto myself; that where I am, there ye may be also" (John 14:3).

Jesus is coming again!

Down through the ages, people have tried to ignore it. But ignoring it won't make it go away.

Even when men were trying their hardest to make it go away, the men and women in this book were whispering the "secret sign," scrawling it on walls, carving it in the catacombs, drawing it in the dirt—

But you don't have to do any of those things.

For the secret's not a secret any more!